THE LION
ENCYCLOPEDIA OF
Christianity

In thanksgiving for the churches of

St George, Altrincham
in the diocese of Chester

and

St Andrew, South Lopham
in the diocese of Norwich

D.S.

THE LION
ENCYCLOPEDIA OF
Christianity

DAVID SELF

LION

A Lion Children's Book
an imprint of
Lion Hudson plc
Wilkinson House, Jordan Hill Road,
Oxford OX2 8DR, England
www.lionhudson.com
UK ISBN 978 0 7459 4949 9
US ISBN 978 0 8254 7808 6

First edition 2007
10 9 8 7 6 5 4 3 2 1

Typeset in 12/15 Latin 725 BT
Printed and bound in Singapore

Distributed by:
UK: Marston Book Services Ltd, PO Box 269, Abingdon, Oxon OX14 4YN
USA: Trafalgar Square Publishing, 814 N Franklin Street, Chicago, IL 60610
USA Christian Market: Kregel Publications, PO Box 2607, Grand Rapids, MI 49501

Acknowledgments
Design by Emma DeBanks.

Text Acknowledgments
Bible extracts, unless otherwise stated, are taken or adapted from the Good News Bible,
published by The Bible Societies/HarperCollins Publishers Ltd, UK © American Bible
Society 1966, 1971, 1976, 1992.

The Bible extracts on pages 29 and 106 are taken from the Holy Bible, New International
Version, copyright © 1973, 1978, 1984 International Bible Society. Used by permission of
Zondervan and Hodder & Stoughton Limited. All rights reserved. The 'NIV' and 'New
International Version' trademarks are registered in the United States Patent and
Trademark Office by International Bible Society. Use of either trademark requires the
permission of International Bible Society. UK trademark number 1448790.

Psalm 23 (on page 77) is from the New Revised Standard Version published by
HarperCollins Publishers, copyright © 1989 by the Division of Christian Education of the
National Council of the Churches of Christ in the USA, and is used by permission. All
rights reserved.

The Apostle's Creed (on page 29) and the Lord's Prayer (on page 71) from Common
Worship: Services and Prayers for the Church of England (Church House Publishing,
2000) are copyright © The English Language Liturgical Consultation, 1988.

Sources:
Chart on page 109: BBC website, figured modified October 2005.
Graph on page 111: US Census Bureau.
Charts on page 119: *Christianity* by Brian Wilson, Routledge, 1999.

Picture Acknowledgments
t=top, b=bottom, c=centre, l=left, r=right

Val Adamson: p. 95t.
Alamy: pp. 6l/Arco Images, 7b/Black Star, 69tl/Thinkstock, 75r/Alan King.
David Alexander: pp. 11t/British Museum; 14l; 22; 36r; 37br.
Jon Arnold Images: p. 30-31b.
Bridgeman Art Library: pp. 8b/Prado, Madrid, Spain, Giraudon; 9t/Church of St.
Therapon, Mytilene, Lesbos, Held Collection; 9r/Palazzo Medici-Riccardi, Florence, Italy;
13/Private Collection; 15t/St Peter the Young, Strasbourg, France, Bildarchiv Steffens;
17c/Galleria degli Uffizi, Florence, Italy, Alinari; 17br/Museum of London, UK;
18/Hamburger Kunsthalle, Hamburg, Germany; 20 and 35/Bibliotheque Nationale, Paris,
France; 23t/Abbey Church of Sant'Antonio di Ranverso, Piedmont, Italy;
27tl/Bibliotheque Sainte-Genevieve, Paris, France, Archives Charmet; 28r/Musee Conde,
Chantilly, France, Lauros, Giraudon; 29/Private Collection, Agnew's, London, UK;
31tr/Musee Marmottan, Paris, France, Giraudon; 33t/Musee Crozatier, Le Puy-en-Velay,
France, Giraudon; 68l/Kremlin Museums, Moscow, Russia; 69tr/Private Collection;
69c/Vatican Museums and Galleries, Vatican City, Italy.
Emma DeBanks: p. 82l.
Werner Forman Archive: p. 34t/National Museum, Copenhagen.
Getty Images: pp. 6b/Tatyana Makeyeva/AFP; 7t/Arif Ali/AFP; 19/Daniel Berehulak;
67br/Tim Graham; 103tl/Hulton Archive.
Sonia Halliday Photographs: pp. 23, 68b.
Lion Hudson: pp. 8cl/bl; 10bl, 36l/David Townsend; 11r; 12; 28l; 30l; 32l; 64l/b; 66bl;
72br; 78; 86cr/Church Missionary Service; 89; 91b; 96br; 101b; 106l.
Rex Nicholls: p. 25br.
Zev Radovan, Jerusalem: pp. 10tl, 90.
Steve Rock: p. 65tr.
Martin Sanders: maps on pp. 21, 32t, 37bl, 44b, 50-51b, 58b; graphics on pp. 22l, 79b,
109b, 111t, 119r.
TopFoto: pp. 51tr/Alinari; 77/Topham Picturepoint; 91t/Reproduced by permission of
HIP; 103tr/The British Library/HIP.
Peter Walker: p. 93t.
Derek West: map on p. 14.

Picture research below courtesy of Zooid Pictures Limited.

AAP (Australian Associated Press): p. 59b/Mick Tsikas.
AKG – Images: pp. 42b-43b; 43tl; 44l; 80l; 81t; 99/Stefan Diller; 117t/Ullstein –
Hoffmann.
Alamy: pp. 3 and 59tl/Lou Linwei; 24l/Charles Bowman; 41r/Homer Sykes; 43tr/Brian
Seed; 45t and 47b/Mary Evans Picture Library; 48b/Ilene MacDonald; 53b/Jon Arnold
Images; 59tr/Popperfoto; 63t/Leslie Garland Picture Library; 72l/Mike Abrahams;
73t/Anders Ryman; 76l/Redferns Music Picture Library; 79br/Philip Scalia; 82b/Yadid
Levy; 87/ArkReligion.com; 88b/Piotr Powietrzynski; 94/Tim Graham; 102/North Wind
Picture Archives; 112 and 119l/Visual Arts Library (London).
ArkReligion.com: pp. 63r/Fiona Good; 71t and 81b/Helene Rogers; 84l/Keith Cardwell.
Bible Society: p. 27r.
Bridgeman Art Library: pp. 73b; 98/British Museum, London, UK.
Circa Photo Library: pp. 109t/William Holtby; 110/John Smith.
Corbis UK Ltd: pp. 40l/Chris Lisle; 40b/Reuters; 41t/Elio Ciol; 42l/Francis G. Mayer; 45ct
and 49/Bettmann; 45b/Patrick Landmann/Sygma; 46t/Gianni Dagli Orti; 46b and
47t/Angelo Hornak; 52b/Wolfgang Kaehler; 55l/Christian Poveda; 56b/David Turnley;
57l/Daniel Lainé; 58t/Bohemian Nomad Picturemakers; 59c/Rolex Dela Pena/Epa;
62b/Joel Stettenheim; 63b/Hanan Isachar; 65b/Archivo Iconografico, S.A.; 70l/Larry
Williams; 71b/Owen Franken; 79t/Douglas Peebles; 79c/Reuters; 80r/Mimmo Jodice;
86b/Jonathan Blair; 88l/Peter Turnley; 92l/Tibor Bognar; 92r/Miguel Vidal/Reuters;
97b/Paul C. Pet/Zefa; 104/Flip Schulke; 107/Peter Kollanyi/Epa; 113/James Davis/Eye
Ubiquitous; 114 and 118/Pizzoli Alberto/Sygma.
The Diocese of Ely: p. 83.
Empics: pp. 84b/PA Wire; 26, 39b, 54, 60b-61b, 108 and 115/Associated Press.
Mary Evans Picture Library: p. 45cb.
Getty Images: pp. 76b/Scott Nelson; 100/Paula Bronstein.
Robert Kawka Photography: p. 67t/Photographers Direct.
KNA-Bild: p. 111.
Howard Koby Photography/Studio 19: p. 60l/Photographers Direct.
Richard Levine and Frances Roberts Stock Photography Research: p.
61r/Photographers Direct.
Christine Osborne Pictures: p. 62t/Photographers Direct.
Photofusion Picture Library: p. 106b/Vehbi Koca.
PictureNet Africa: p. 56l/Nadine Hutton.
Rex Features: pp. 39r/Action Press; 93r/Paul Cooper.
St Christopher's Hospice: p. 101/Brian Harris.
Staatsbibliothek Bamberg: p. 34b.
Still Pictures: pp. 55r/Russell Gordon; 70r/Sean Sprague.
TopFoto: pp. 52t; 53t/Image Works; 57r; 97t/Alinari; 105/Steven Rubin/The Image
Works.
World Council of Churches: pp. 116/Pete Williams; 117r.
World Religions Photo Library: p. 95b/Photographers Direct/Claire Stout; 96l/Christine
Osborne/Photographers Direct.

Contents

It all began with Jesus. His many followers called themselves Christians.

The Crystal Cathedral in Los Angeles, USA, is a modern building that celebrates the Christian faith.

Changing the World

Through its followers, Christianity has done a lot to change the way people live. Many countries' laws are based on Christian teaching. The message of Jesus has inspired many politicians, explorers and scientists. It has led people to compose glorious music, to create wonderful works of art and to write great books.

This faith has led others to build schools and colleges and to work as nurses, doctors and teachers. Others have started charities, nursing homes and hospitals – or given money to help others to do such good works.

1 A Worldwide Faith

Christianity is one of the world's great religions. Not only that: it is the one with the most followers – and it all began with one man in a small Middle Eastern country. For just three years, that man journeyed around his homeland, teaching and healing. Then he was executed by being nailed to a cross. His name was Jesus. Two thousand years later, his name is known all around the world.

Over the years, his message spread across Europe. Out of that teaching has grown a worldwide faith with believers in every continent around the world. In fact there are now far more Christians in central and southern America than in Europe. There are also millions of believers in Africa, Asia and North America. No less than one third of the world's population claims to be Christian.

These Christians may seem to have very little in common with one another. For example, a church service in Russia may be very different from one in Africa. Indeed, over the years, Christians have separated into over 20,000 different groups or denominations. These groups have sometimes quarrelled between themselves. Indeed, Christians have sometimes fought and even killed each other because they have disagreed with one other.

A girl lights a candle in an Orthodox church in Russia.

Look it Up

25 The Church in Central and South America
45 Helping Others

These Pakistani children hold candles to express their hope that God will help them through troubled times – in this case, a shattering earthquake.

Despite their differences, Christians all believe in the one God, and they all try to follow the teachings and example of the same Jesus Christ who came to be a kind of light in the world that would show them the way to live their lives.

Members of this church in Ghana enthusiastically sing their praise of God.

Christians believe that Jesus was a human being but also that God was his father.

The Messiah

It was only some years after Jesus' death that his followers became known as Christians. This name came about because Jesus was also called 'the Christ'. Christ is not a name but a Greek title which means 'the anointed one' or 'the chosen one'.

The Hebrew word for this is 'messiah'.

Jesus has been known to his followers as the Messiah since the time he was alive on earth.

משיח

Hebrew is written (and therefore read) from right to left. It is usual to show only consonants; the reader is supposed to know which vowels to say.

2 The Son of God

For Christians, the centre of their faith is the man called Jesus. We know he was a real person because of another man called Flavius Josephus. Josephus was a Jewish writer and a Pharisee. Later, he became a Roman citizen, which made him an important person. In his books, he wrote about Jesus and his followers.

But we know very little of Jesus apart from the writings of Josephus and what was written about Jesus by his own followers.

In the stories or 'Gospels' that four of his followers have left us, we are told that his mother was called Mary and her husband was called Joseph. When Jesus was about 30, he started journeying around the district, known as Galilee, teaching and healing. Then, after three years, he went south to the capital of his country, the city of Jerusalem.

In less than a week, the crowds there turned against him. At the end of that week he was put to death like a criminal by being nailed to a cross.

Despite his short life, Jesus was not forgotten. His already-devoted followers dedicated themselves to spreading the news of his life and teaching, and he now has millions of followers around the world. To them, he is special in a way no other person is.

Luke's Gospel in the Bible tells of the angel Gabriel's announcement to Mary that she was to be the mother of Jesus. Paintings of the Annunciation often show Mary being touched by a shaft of light from heaven.

This stylized Greek Orthodox painting of Jesus is called an icon.

Body and Soul

Christians believe that each person consists of a body and soul. The body is what we can see: our bones, flesh and blood. The soul can't be seen and surgeons can't find it inside a body in the way they can find the brain.

For Christians, the soul is that inner part of the human: the part that makes each person different and the part which (they believe) lives for ever – even after the death of the body.

Some Christians say their soul is saved through belief in Jesus.

Other Christians say their soul will be saved by the way they live their lives on earth.

Christians believe that, after death, their souls will go to be with God and the angels in heaven.

Jesus' followers believe that he was fully human and experienced all the sorrow and happiness of everyday life in the same way that other people did in his time. But while they believe his mother was a woman called Mary, they believe his father was not Joseph but God himself. Their belief is that, in a mysterious way, Mary was made pregnant by God. Jesus, they say, was the Son of God. In Jesus, God had come to earth.

One day, while Jesus was travelling around, he asked his twelve closest friends, 'Who do you say that I am?' One of them, a fisherman called Peter, answered, 'You are… the Son of the living God.' (Matthew 16:16.)

That is still the answer many Christians give when asked who they think Jesus was. Their belief is that God became a human being, living on earth as Jesus. He did this, they say, for a very special reason. They believe that not only did Jesus live and die on earth but, three days after his death, he came back to life. He 'rose from the dead'.

Christians say that, in this way, Jesus proved that death is not the end of everything but a new beginning: the start of a new life after death. They also believe that, by dying on the cross, Jesus saved human beings from the results of their wrongdoings or 'sins'.

Look it Up

Jesus was born a Jew and grew up in the Jewish faith.

3 The Beginning of Christianity

From all that we know, Jesus' earthly parents were very religious. When he was a boy, they took him to the Jewish temple in Jerusalem. As a grown-up, he went to a Jewish place of worship (called a synagogue) on the Jewish holy day of the week – which is called the sabbath. The Jewish sabbath begins at dusk on Friday and ends at dusk on Saturday.

So for all those who follow Jesus, the teachings of Judaism (the religion of the Jews) are also important – so important that when the early Christians began to compile their own book of holy writings (which is called the Bible), they included in it the collection of Jewish holy books called the Tenakh. Christians know these books as the 'Old Testament'.

This scroll of Jewish scriptures, written in Hebrew, dates from around 30–50 CE. The scroll contains a selection from the book of Psalms.

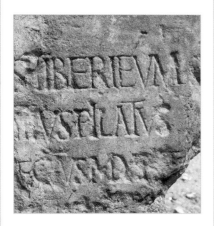

The second line of this inscription, found on a stone slab in Caesarea, shows the latter part of the name Pontius Pilatus – clear evidence that Pontius Pilate is truly a figure from history.

Who Were the Jews?

The land of the Jewish people lies at the eastern end of the Mediterranean Sea. Its boundaries and its name have changed many times. Much of it now forms part of the modern state of Israel. Christians often call it the 'Holy Land'.

In biblical times (just as in modern times), it was a land that had often been fought over. Once it was invaded by tribes known as the Philistines. Many stories are told of this period: how, for example, a Jewish shepherd boy called David killed a Philistine champion, a giant of a man called Goliath, with a single shot from his sling or catapult.

Later, the northern part of the country was invaded by a people called the Assyrians. The citizens of the north were exiled and dispersed. Many of the Jewish people who lived there moved south to the area known as Judah or Judea. At its centre was what had become the Jews' most important city, Jerusalem. Even today, Jerusalem is a very special and holy place for all Jews – as it has also become for Christians. Later, it became important for Muslims, the followers of the religion called Islam.

A few hundred years after the Assyrian invasion, the Jews were attacked again – this time from the east by Babylonians. Many were taken to Babylon as captives. On their return, they set about rebuilding their capital city, Jerusalem.

By the time Jesus was born, the Romans had taken control of all the countries around the Mediterranean Sea. This mighty empire was

This Assyrian carving, showing the defeat of the city of Lachish, is one of very few pictures of a Bible event. The Israelites did not make pictures of themselves, as they believed God's laws forbade it.

Look it Up

2 The Son of God
11 The Christian Bible

The Pharisees

Just as there are different groupings or denominations of Christians, so there were different groups among Jews in the time of Jesus. One group was the Pharisees. They spent much time in the study of Jewish laws and tried to keep these laws strictly. Many Pharisees were very holy but some were not as good as they claimed. At first they agreed with Jesus' teaching but later turned against him.

Pharisees took special care to hang long tassles on the corners of their prayer shawls – in strict obedience to the Jewish laws.

ruled from Rome, by its emperor, but in each part there was a local governor. At the time of Jesus' birth, the local ruler in Jerusalem was a Jew known as King Herod the Great. He was unpopular with his own people for siding with the Roman invaders. By the time of Jesus' crucifixion, he had been replaced by another Roman governor, Pontius Pilate, who probably came from Spain – which was also part of the empire.

In the time of Jesus, the Jews were hoping to be freed from Roman rule. They thought this might be brought about by a new religious leader whom they called 'the Messiah'.

Jewish Beliefs

Most of the peoples in neighbouring countries (and the Romans) believed in many gods. They believed, for example, that there were separate gods of the sun and sea and a goddess of love. Over the years, the Jews had come to believe in just one God who made heaven and earth.

This is God who is written about in the Jewish Bible (the Old Testament), God who was spoken of by Jesus and whom he called 'Father'. Christians worship and respect the same God.

The Jews had learned about God from their holy men or prophets and other leaders. The most famous of these was Moses. Books in the Old Testament are named after others such as Samuel, Jeremiah and Isaiah. All these prophets were important to Jesus – and therefore are important to Christians.

**Christians celebrate the
birth of Jesus each year
at Christmas.**

Christmas Celebrations

Most Christians go to church
at Christmas, many going to a
special midnight service as
Christmas Eve becomes
Christmas Day to celebrate the
'Nativity' or birth of Jesus.
Many Christians give presents
at this time and some act out
the story of the first Christmas
in what are called Nativity
plays. Others will arrange
models to create a picture
of the scene in Bethlehem.

Members of the Orthodox
Church celebrate Christmas
Day on 7 January.

Although the stories in Luke and Matthew's
Gospels differ, Nativity plays and scenes often
include details from both – such as the arrival of
both shepherds and wise men to visit the baby
Jesus.

4 The First Christmas

The story of the birth of Jesus is told in only two of the four Gospels
in the New Testament and those two tell us different things about the
birth.

In his Gospel, Luke tells how a young woman called Mary was
visited by an angel and told that she would give birth to a son. The
father of the child would not be Joseph, the man to whom she was
engaged, nor indeed any man. The child's father was to be God
himself.

At that time, the Romans held a census (a count) so they knew how
many people should be taxed. To do this, they made everybody return
to their family home. Although Mary and Joseph lived in Nazareth,
Joseph's family came from Bethlehem, a small town 120 miles (190
kilometres) to the south. They made the journey there and, while they
were there, Mary gave birth. Luke tells how the first people to visit the
baby were shepherds who had been guarding their sheep on a nearby
hillside and who had been told to visit the child by angels.

Matthew tells how 'wise men' from the east later came to visit the
child. Matthew also tells us they brought three presents:
- gold, which is usually a gift for a king
- sweet-smelling frankincense or incense, a sign of holiness
- myrrh, which is a precious ointment used before burials and a
sign of suffering.

Some people call the wise men 'kings' and say there were three of
them because they brought three gifts.

Christmas

In much of the world, Christmas Day happens on 25 December but the
first Christmas Day almost certainly wasn't in December. December is
a rainy time of the year in that part of the world so it is unlikely that
the Romans would have held the census then or that shepherds would
keep their sheep out overnight.

By the year 354 CE, Christmas was being celebrated on 25 December.
The early Church may have chosen that date because it was already a
holiday throughout the Roman empire. It celebrated the facts that the
shortest day of the winter was over and the days were now
getting lighter. The Church used this holiday to teach that
Jesus was a new light in the world.

A Jewish Belief

The Jewish prophets taught that God would send a 'Messiah' or 'Chosen One' to earth. He would save the Jewish people from their enemies. He would put an end to their suffering and bring about a new age of peace and holiness.

Some Jews were expecting the Messiah to come at the time Jesus was born – partly because their land had been invaded by the Romans and many were suffering. When Jesus grew up, some Jews believed he was the Messiah but most did not.

Christians believe several passages in the Old Testament show that Jesus was the Messiah. For example:

'The Lord says, "Bethlehem, you are one of the smallest towns in Judah, but out of you I will bring a ruler for Israel." '
Micah 5:2

'The blind will be able to see, and the deaf will hear. The lame will leap and dance, and those who cannot speak will shout for joy.'
Isaiah 35:5–6

'Shout for joy, you people of Jerusalem! Look, your king is coming to you! He comes triumphant… but humble and riding on a donkey.'
Zechariah 9:9

John's Gospel says that Jesus was the light of the world. Many classical paintings of the Nativity scene, like this one, show light shining from the baby's crib.

Look it Up

2 The Son of God
37 The Christian Year

With his followers, Jesus spent three years journeying around, teaching and healing.

Miracles

Jesus' acts of healing (many of which seemed to go against the laws of nature or science) are known as miracles. Jesus also performed other miracles. One story tells how he fed 5000 people with just a few loaves and fishes.

Many Christians believe these miracles happened just as they are described in the Bible. Some believe there may be another explanation but all agree that they were written in the belief that Jesus was 'special'.

This ancient mosaic of loaves and fishes, from a church in Galilee, remembers the miracle Jesus performed in feeding the 5000.

Look it Up

7 The First Christians
9 The Teachings of Jesus

5 The Ministry of Jesus

After Jesus was born in Bethlehem in Judea, his parents went back north to their home in Nazareth where his earthly father, Joseph, was a carpenter and (probably) a builder. Jesus may well have learned the same trades. Nazareth was in a province called Galilee. Both Galilee and Judea were part of the mighty Roman empire.

Joseph and Mary were devout Jews and Jesus went to the local synagogue on the Jewish holy day or sabbath. When he grew up, he was asked to read and preach in the local synagogue so he must have been able to read and write.

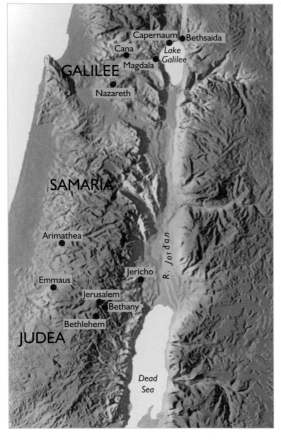

When he was about 30, he moved to Capernaum and chose 12 local men to be his closest followers or disciples. With them, he spent three years journeying around Galilee and nearby areas, talking to and teaching the people they met.

Besides these 12 men, Jesus had many other close friends and followers who are also sometimes known as disciples. Among them were several women, including a woman from Magdala named Mary.

This period of time is called his 'ministry', meaning the time he 'served' and cared for his people.

Jesus the Healer

Some of the people who came to listen brought others who were ill, disabled or mentally ill. The Bible says that Jesus cured many of these people including: a paralysed man; sufferers from leprosy; the deaf, dumb and blind; and a boy suffering from epileptic fits.

Sometimes Jesus cured them by touch or by the use of saliva (known in those days as having the power to cure). Other times, he cured people by telling them their sins or wrongdoings were forgiven.

On more than one occasion, the person was cured simply by their faith in Jesus.

In those days, a range of illnesses that produced puzzling behaviour in their vicims were attributed to demon possession. The Gospels say that Jesus cured such people by commanding the devils to come out of them.

In modern times, some churches have carried on Jesus' ministry of healing by holding special healing services. These may be simple services of prayer or they may include anointing with oil as a sign of blessing. At other services, a minister or other healer may command evil spirits to leave a sick person. Not every Christian church does this.

Jesus called his first disciples 'fishers of men' because four of them had been fishermen before they agreed to follow Jesus. This wall painting shows the disciples in Peter's ship during the storm on Lake Galilee.

From the earliest days of Christianity, Jesus' followers have continued to work for healing as Jesus did. The Bible tells the story of Peter and John healing a lame beggar on the steps of the Temple.

The Disciples

The twelve men Jesus chose to be his disciples were:

Simon, whom Jesus named Peter

Andrew, who was Simon Peter's brother

James and **John**, who were also brothers and who both (like Simon Peter and Andrew) had been fishermen on the Sea of Galilee until Jesus 'called' them to be disciples (Simon Peter, James and John seem to have been the closest followers of Jesus)

Philip

Bartholomew, surnamed Nathanael

Thomas, who was a twin and who also doubted that Jesus had risen from the dead until he saw and touched him for himself

Matthew, who had been a tax collector working for the Romans until he was called by Jesus

James the Less (so called so as not to confuse him with James the brother of John)

Thaddaeus, also known in the New Testament as Jude

Simon (known as the Patriot)

Judas Iscariot, who betrayed Jesus and then committed suicide.

When Jesus left his disciples to return to heaven, he 'sent them out' to share his teaching around the world. For this reason, we also describe the disciples as 'apostles' – meaning 'those who are sent'.

The days leading up Jesus' death are known as Holy Week.

6 The Death and Resurrection of Jesus

Having spent three years teaching and healing, Jesus and his followers journeyed to Jerusalem. He entered the city riding on a donkey – as the prophet Zechariah had said the Messiah would (Zechariah 9:9).

Large crowds welcomed him, waving branches of palm trees. For this reason, Christians named this day Palm Sunday.

Jesus spent the week living with friends in a nearby village called Bethany. Each day he went into Jerusalem and taught in the Temple, the Jews' most holy building. Because he was so popular, some of the Jewish religious leaders began to be jealous of him and were concerned he was turning people against them. They also disliked what he was saying so they began to plot how to stop him.

They were helped when one of his disciples, Judas, offered to betray Jesus.

The Last Supper

On the Thursday evening, Jesus had a 'last supper' with his disciples. During the evening, he washed their feet (a sign that he was their servant) and commanded them to eat bread and drink wine in his memory. In the account given by John, Jesus told them, 'A new commandment I give you: Love one another.' That command gives the day its name: Maundy Thursday ('Maundy' from the Latin word for 'command').

Judas left the meal to tell the priests where Jesus would be later that evening.

After their meal, Jesus and his disciples went into a garden to pray. Judas led soldiers belonging to the priests there and there they arrested Jesus.

Circular timeline labels (clockwise from top):
Dawn: Jesus found guilty by High Priests
6am: Jesus is taken to Pilate
9am: Jesus is taken away to be crucified
Noon: Jesus is nailed to the cross
3pm: Jesus dies
5pm: Jesus is buried in the tomb

Timeline of the Crucifixion
The events of that day probably happened at about these times:
Dawn: Jesus found guilty by High Priests.
6am: Jesus is taken to Pilate.
9am: Jesus is taken away to be crucified.
Noon: Jesus is nailed to the cross.
3pm: Jesus dies.
5pm: Jesus is buried just before the Jewish sabbath begins. This particular sabbath was very special for Jews as it was part of a festival called Passover.

The Crucifixion

Jesus was put on trial by the priests. They found him guilty of blasphemy (preaching against God) but, as they did not have the authority to put him to death, they sent him to the Roman governor of the country, Pontius Pilate. He found no fault with Jesus.

By now the priests had the people on their side and a mob was chanting for the death of Jesus. To prevent a riot, Pilate ordered him to be beaten and put to death by being nailed to a wooden cross. After three hours on the cross, Jesus died. His body was taken down and placed in a small cave and a heavy stone rolled across the entrance.

That happened on the day Christians now call Good Friday. One reason why this day is named 'Good' is that, although it commemorates a sorrowful event, it is 'good' because Easter could not happen without the crucifixion. However, the English name 'Good Friday' probably comes from an old name for the day: 'God's Friday'.

A striking depiction of Jesus rising from the ground by the Italian artist Botticelli (1445–1510).

Easter Morning

So ended the week. Then, on the Sunday morning, one or more of the women who had been among his followers (who included Mary, the mother of James and John, and Mary from Magdala) went to the tomb. They found the stone had been rolled away and were told by an angel that Jesus had risen from the dead. They ran to tell his disciples and, later, Peter and John also found that the tomb was empty. These events of that Sunday are remembered by Christians every Sunday and especially on the Sunday at the end of Holy Week, named Easter Sunday.

Over the next forty days, Jesus appeared on several occasions to different groups of his followers. From these accounts, Christians have come to believe that Jesus did indeed rise from the dead – an event they call his Resurrection.

Look it Up

34 Holy Communion
37 The Christian Year

Remembering Holy Week

Each year, in the week before Easter, many Christians recall the events of Holy Week in special ways.

Palm Sunday

When Christians go to church on this day, they may receive small crosses, made out of folded strips of palm – as reminders of the joy of the first Palm Sunday but also of how the crowds later demanded Jesus' death by crucifixion.

Maundy Thursday

Many churches hold services of Holy Communion to remember the Last Supper Jesus had with his disciples and the new commandment he gave them.

Good Friday

In many churches, the main service on Good Friday takes place between midday and three o'clock (the hours Jesus is said to have hung on the cross).
In some places there are processions of witness, or re-enactments of the crucifixion.

Depictions of the cross or crucifix are popular in Christian art. By making these artefacts in precious metals and jewels, Christians express how important the crucifixion is in their faith.

Jesus' followers believed that, 50 days after Easter, God sent his Holy Spirit to them.

7  The First Christians

Jesus was put to death for being a possible rebel leader. On Easter Day, his followers became convinced he was alive again. Forty days later, he left them to return to heaven. This event is called the Ascension.

Seven weeks (or 50 days) after Easter, his followers met in an upstairs room in Jerusalem. As they were praying, they heard a sound like 'the rush of a mighty wind'. They saw what looked like tongues of fire on their heads but were unharmed. From this sign, they realized that Jesus' promise to send them (and all his followers) a source of strength and comfort, which he called the Holy Spirit, had come true.

The New Apostle

Between Easter and Pentecost, the followers of Jesus met to pray and to choose a new disciple or apostle to take the place of Judas Iscariot, who had betrayed Jesus. They chose a man called Matthias.

Simon Peter

When Jesus first called the brothers Simon and Andrew to be disciples, he said to Simon, 'I shall call you Kephas.' *Kephas* was the word for 'rock' in Aramaic. When the Gospel story was written down, it was written in Greek and the Greek word for rock is *petra* – so Simon became known as Petros or Peter.

Later in his ministry, Jesus said to Peter:

'You are a rock and on this rock foundation I will build my church.'

Matthew 16:18

Because of this, Peter became one of the leaders of the first Christians. In the years ahead, he did much to spread the teachings of Jesus and journeyed to many places.

Later, there was some disagreement among Christians as to whether the message of Jesus was meant only for Jewish people or for all people. Peter argued very strongly that anyone could become a Christian: you didn't have first to be Jewish (as most of the first followers of Jesus had been).

Finally, Peter travelled to Rome. In later times, he was considered to be the first Bishop of Rome.

It has become traditional in Christian art to depict Peter with elaborate keys as Jesus told him that he was going to give him the keys to the kingdom of heaven.

They rushed into the streets to preach and to persuade people to follow the teachings of Jesus. This was the first time they had done this – until then fearing that the Jews or Romans would punish them as they had punished Jesus. Some of the crowds who heard them thought they were drunk even though it was early morning. But foreigners in the city understood what they were saying, though the words they were heard to speak were in different languages.

That day, it is said, 3000 people became Christians. For this reason, the day is sometimes called the birthday (or the start) of the Christian Church.

Look it Up

29 The Clergy of the Church
37 The Christian Year

Stephen, the First Martyr

In the early days of the church in Jerusalem, the disciples (or apostles) chose seven men to be their helpers or 'deacons'. The first of these was a young man called Stephen. He spoke in defence of the followers of Jesus to the Jewish council and, as a result, was condemned to death by stoning. He became the first person to be killed or martyred for his Christian beliefs.

Pentecost

The day the Holy Spirit came to the disciples was a Jewish festival called Pentecost. It was called Pentecost, because it occurs 50 days after the Passover, *pente* coming from the Greek word for 50. Christians named their own festival marking the coming of the Holy Spirit 'Pentecost' – because it happened 50 days after Easter. The Jewish and Christian Pentecost festivals do not always happen on the same day because Passover and Easter do not always happen at the same weekend. A traditional British name for Pentecost is Whitsun.

Pentecost is remembered in the mitre (or flame-shaped headdress) worn by bishops, the successors of the original apostles. This archbishop's extremely decorative vestments evoke the wind and fire of the first Pentecost.

The person who first took the teaching of Jesus to non-Jews is known as Paul.

Look it Up

10 The Teachings of Paul

This ninth-century painting shows scenes from the life of St Paul, including the blinding light of his conversion, his learning from another Christian in Damascus and his preaching.

8 The Life and Journeys of Paul

The Pharisees had been keen to stop Jesus spreading his teaching to the people of Jerusalem. Following the crucifixion of Jesus, a young man called Saul was still eager to discover and bring to trial any of Jesus' followers. He was one of those who watched the stoning to death of Stephen.

Later, Saul journeyed from Jerusalem to Damascus to hunt out Christians there.

On his way, Saul had a vision of Jesus. He fell to the ground and heard a voice saying, 'Saul, Saul, why do you persecute me?' When Saul staggered to his feet, he realized he was now blind – so his companions led him into Damascus. There, a Christian called Ananias visited him, put his hands on his head and told him Jesus had sent him to Saul. At that moment, Saul's sight returned. He was baptized as a Christian. In future, he was known by the Roman version of his name, Paul.

After becoming a believer in Jesus, Paul returned to Jerusalem. Not surprisingly, the followers of Jesus in Jerusalem were highly suspicious. One of them, called Barnabas, had heard what had happened in Damascus and spoke up for him. Paul stayed in Jerusalem, preaching the message of Jesus. This annoyed some of his original friends among the Pharisees – so much so that his life was in danger. He went back to his home in Tarsus.

Around the year 45 CE, a group of Christians in a town called Antioch, which is between Tarsus and Jerusalem, decided the message of Jesus should be spread to other

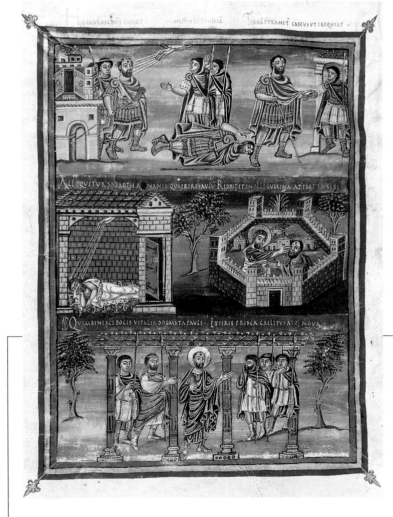

Who Was Paul?

- He was born in Tarsus
- He was a Greek-speaking Jew
- He was a freeborn citizen of the Roman empire (which gave him many privileges)
- His job was making tents and sails for ships
- He was a Pharisee

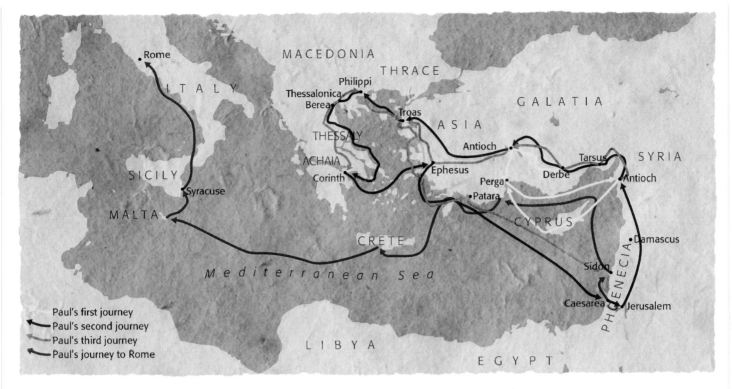

countries. They chose Paul (who could speak Greek, the language spoken in many of the places he would visit) and also Barnabas to do this work.

In the following years, Paul travelled round the Mediterranean, spreading the teachings of Jesus. After three long journeys, he returned to Jerusalem. His preaching there caused problems and disagreements between Jews and those who had become Christians. One disagreement turned into a riot and the Roman authorities put Paul in prison. As a Roman, Paul claimed the right to be tried in Rome. He was eventually sent there.

Paul died in Rome at about the same time as Peter, who had also journeyed to Rome to spread Jesus' teachings.

On all his travels, Paul preached to Jews and non-Jews (or 'Gentiles') about Jesus. Among these was an important, wealthy woman called Lydia. She may have been the first person in Europe to become a Christian. Many other women were among those Paul taught about Jesus.

Like Peter, Paul felt that Gentiles who became Christians needn't follow Jewish ways and customs, such as going to the Jewish synagogue.

For this reason and because he was the first apostle to spread the Christian message outside Palestine, Paul is known as the Apostle to the Gentiles.

Paul's Journeys

In 46–47, Paul went by ship to Cyprus and then on to Asia Minor (now southern Turkey). He returned by sea.

In 50–52, he went overland to his home town of Tarsus, then right across Asia Minor. From a city called Troas, he went by ship to Greece and then south to Corinth. He then returned to Ephesus in Asia Minor and sailed back to Caesarea.

In 52–56, he journeyed by land from Syria to Ephesus, and then by sea to northern Greece. He went south to Corinth and then back north by almost the same route. He then sailed back to Palestine.

His final journey in 60 was to Rome as a prisoner, sailing first to Crete, then towards Italy, being shipwrecked on Malta. He was taken to Sicily and then Rome.

The teachings of Jesus have always been the most important part of the Christian faith.

The Four Gospels

Four stories or accounts survive of the life and teachings of Jesus. These are called 'Gospels' and are part of the Christian Bible. We do not know for sure who wrote these four Gospels although they are named after men who might have written them.

- Matthew: one of the twelve disciples of Jesus
- Mark: a young man who knew Peter, another disciple
- Luke: a Greek doctor who may not have met Jesus but who knew Paul
- John: probably the youngest of the twelve disciples of Jesus

Mark's Gospel is the shortest and was the first to be written. The writers of Matthew and Luke included many stories from that Gospel.

Some of the things Jesus said and did are included in all or several of the Gospels but each writer also included things the others did not. The word 'Gospel' means 'good news'.

The road from Jerusalem to Jericho.

Look it Up

33 Private and Public Prayer (The Lord's Prayer), 34 Holy Communion

9 The Teachings of Jesus

Jesus spent much of his time during the three years of his ministry teaching and talking to people who came to listen – either in synagogues on the Jewish sabbath or 'holy day', in people's homes or out of doors.

For two thousand years, his followers have tried to be true to his teachings. Even today, when faced with a new problem or question a Christian may think, 'What would Jesus have said – or done?' They pray as he taught them to do – and go to a church service called Holy Communion, as he commanded them to do. Their church service of Holy Communion is a memorial of Jesus' last supper with his disciples.

Jesus also taught that there were two great commandments: 'Love God' and 'Love your neighbour as yourself'.

Although all Christians try to follow his teachings, not all succeed. Christians believe God will forgive their failings – if they honestly want to do better.

Parables

Jesus often taught people by telling them parables or 'stories with a meaning'. When he told his followers that it was important to love their neighbour, a lawyer asked him, 'Who is my neighbour?' Jesus answered by telling a story.

A Jewish man travelling to Jericho was attacked by robbers. Two other Jews ignored him as he lay wounded. Then a man from Samaria came along. Most Jews looked down on the people of Samaria. Even so, this Samaritan looked after the Jewish person who had been attacked and paid for him to rest in an inn or hotel. Jesus ended by asking which of the three had been 'a good neighbour'.

When the lawyer answered, 'the one who had been good to him', Jesus simply said, 'Go and do the same.' (Luke 10:30–37.)

Forty of the parables told by Jesus are recorded in the Gospels, some of them in more than one Gospel.

Christian teachers still talk about the meanings or messages all the parables continue to have for present-day followers of Jesus.

The Sermon on the Mount

The writer of Matthew's Gospel collected together many of Jesus' sayings and arranged them together. He says that Jesus addressed the crowds on a hillside, and the readings are often known as the 'Sermon on the Mount'.

In it, Jesus taught that people should not only believe in God but should worship him – and try to do what God wants for them. But Jesus also said many things that surprised his listeners. These included not only 'loving your neighbour' but loving and forgiving your enemies.

Also included in the Sermon on the Mount are some sayings (known as the Beatitudes) in which Jesus stated which people are happy or 'blessed'. These are four of the Beatitudes from Matthew's Gospel (5:3–10):

A fresco or wall painting in an Italian church of St John the Evangelist.

- *Blessed are the poor in spirit, for theirs is the kingdom of heaven.*

- *Blessed are those who mourn, for they will be comforted.*

- *Blessed are those who hunger and thirst for righteousness, for they will be filled.*

- *Blessed are those who are persecuted because of righteousness, for theirs is the kingdom of heaven.*

This church on a hillside near Capernaum is near the place Jesus is said to have given his 'Sermon on the Mount'. It is called the Church of the Beatitudes.

Paul took the teachings of Jesus to many other countries and people.

Epistles to the Corinthians

Corinth is a seaport in Greece. After he had visited the city, Paul wrote two letters to his Christian friends there.

His first letter begins with an announcement of who it is from:

From Paul, who was called by the will of God to be an apostle of Christ Jesus, and from our brother Sosthenes…

We think Sosthenes was the leader of a Jewish synagogue in Corinth who had become a Christian and moved to Ephesus (from where Paul was writing the letter). Paul next greets the Corinthian Christians:

To the church of God which is in Corinth, to all who are called to be God's holy people, who belong to him in union with Christ Jesus.

10 The Teachings of Paul

Paul is important to Christians because he played a very great part in spreading the news about Jesus beyond the land where Jesus lived and to non-Jews (Gentiles). He is also remembered because of the letters (known as epistles) he wrote to those he met on his travels around the Mediterranean. These epistles include Paul's teachings about Jesus. Thirteen of them survive as part of the New Testament.

Eight were written while he was on his second and third of his great missionary journeys around the empire. For instance, while he was staying in Ephesus, he wrote to the Christians in Corinth whom he had visited earlier. Paul probably dictated his letters to a friend or secretary who wrote them down. When he added a personal note, he had to apologize for his handwriting (Galatians 6:11).

Some of Paul's letters are not easy to understand. One reason is that many are replies to letters Paul had received. Reading them is like listening to one end of a telephone conversation and having to guess what is being said at the other end.

It is easy to imagine Paul walking up and down a room, dictating the letters at high speed. Sometimes he goes off his subject as he thinks of something else to say – before coming back to his main point.

In many of his letters, Paul teaches that Jesus was 'God made flesh' or 'God incarnate': the fact that God allowed himself in the form of Jesus to be put to death on the cross shows how great God's love is for all people. Paul also teaches that, by suffering and dying on the cross, Jesus took on himself the punishment for all our wrongdoings rather than have his followers suffer.

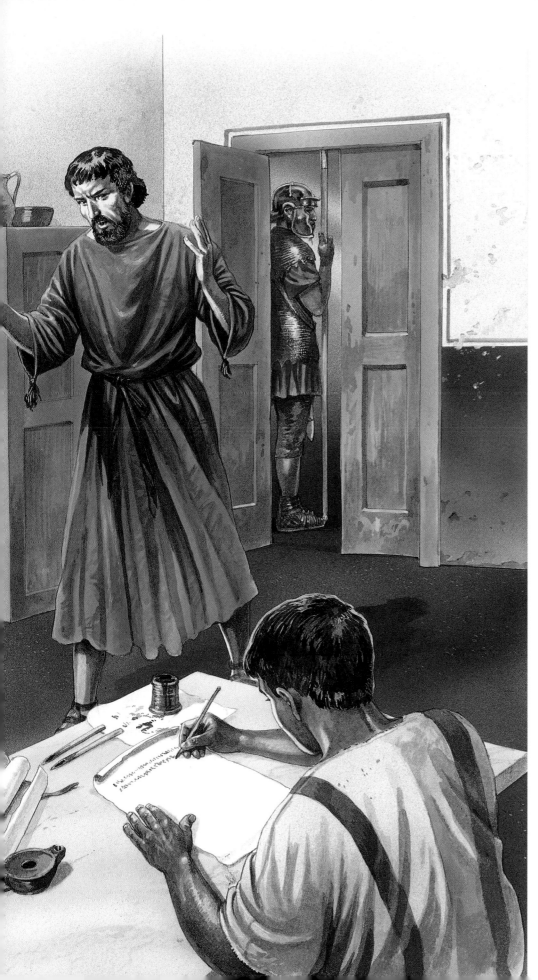

The Letter to Philemon

While he was awaiting trial in Rome, Paul was not kept in prison but under 'house arrest'. That meant he was allowed to rent his own house, but was kept in chains inside it, under the guard of a Roman soldier. He was allowed visitors – and allowed to write and send letters.

One of these letters was a very short one sent to a man called Philemon who lived in Colassae and had become a Christian when Paul preached there. Like many rich people in those times (including Christians), Philemon owned a number of slaves. One of his slaves was called Onesimos (or Onesimus).

Onesimos had run away to Rome, met Paul and become a Christian. He became very useful to Paul, running errands and doing other jobs. Eventually Paul decided he should send Onesimos back to Philemon – with an 'Epistle to Philemon'. In this letter, Paul asks Philemon to receive Onesimos not as a slave but as a brother and fellow Christian.

Look it Up

8 The Life and Journeys of Paul
49 Christian Reformers

25

For Christians, the most important book in the world is the Bible.

11 The Christian Bible

The Bible is not just one book but a whole library of books written over a period of a thousand years. The word 'Bible' comes from a Greek noun *Ta Biblia* meaning 'the books'.

It is divided into two parts called 'Testaments'. The word 'testament' means promise or agreement. The first or Old Testament contains 39 separate books including histories, law books, poetry, prophecies, songs and stories. These books, arranged in a slightly different order, also form the Jewish bible or Tenakh. It was mostly written in Hebrew, the old language of the Jews. By Jesus' time, it had also been translated into Aramaic, the language he spoke.

The second or New Testament contains 27 books written during the 100 years following the death of Jesus. They were written in Greek, which was then the language most widely spoken around the eastern end of the Mediterranean.

The first four books of the New Testament are the Gospels. These may have been written as late as 70 CE, by which time the people who had actually known Jesus were dying and it was important to have a written record of what he had said and done.

The Apocrypha

When people were deciding which books should be kept within the Bible, there was disagreement. Many Christians, including Roman Catholics, accept a number of books about the Jews and their beliefs (written between BCE 300 and 100 CE) which had been important in the centuries up to and including the time of Jesus but were not included in the final Jewish selection of scriptures. Centuries later, reforming Christians decided to leave them out of their Bible. In some Christian Bibles they are printed as part of the Old Testament. In other Bibles they are printed separately between the Testaments and called either the Apocrypha (which means 'the hidden things') or the Deuterocanon.

Following the Gospels is another book said to have been written by Luke, one of the first Gentiles to become a Christian. It is called the Acts of the Apostles and describes the early years of the Church and also Paul's travels.

Following these five books are letters or epistles written by the earliest Christians – Paul, Peter, John and other apostles.

The last book of the New Testament is called the Revelation and is a poetic vision or dream of how God will finally put right the troubles of the world.

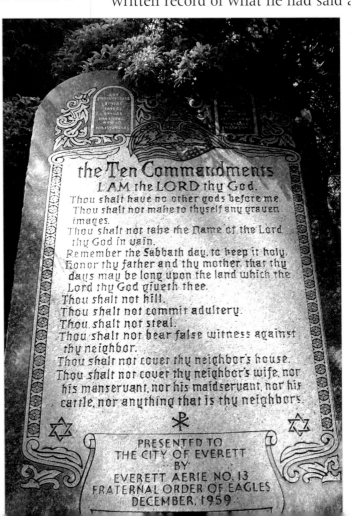

The Ten Commandments are carved into this monument in a town called Everett in the state of Washington, USA.

Before the invention of printing, copies of the Bible were made by hand. The monks who did this work would spend hours creating beautifully decorated lettering and illustrations. This one, from fourteenth century France, shows Noah releasing the dove.

How the Bible Came to Us

In the early years of the Church there was much discussion whether other Gospels and epistles should have been included, but in the year 376, a bishop called Athanasius produced the list of books we now call the New Testament. By now, parts of it had been translated into Latin, the language of the Roman empire. In the year 382, the pope at that time, a man called Damasus I, asked a very clever Christian called Jerome to translate the whole Bible into Latin from Hebrew and Greek. The 'Jerome Bible' is known as the Vulgate from a Latin word meaning 'in common use'.

Only after the Reformation was the complete Bible translated into modern European languages – and, years later, into non-European languages.

How Christians Read the Bible

Christians believe the Bible is a 'message' from God that teaches not only what God is like but also how believers should live their lives. The Old Testament is important because it is the Bible Jesus knew but most Christians believe the New Testament is more important because it contains the life and teachings of Jesus himself.

The Bible for the World

In the year 1794, a ten-year-old Welsh girl called Mary Jones so wanted to read the Bible in her own language, Welsh, that she saved up for the next six years. One day she heard some were for sale in a town several miles away. She made the long walk over the mountains and, although they had all been sold by the time she got there, she was eventually given one.

People in London heard her story and in 1804 they started the British and Foreign Bible Society, now called the Bible Society. In the 200 years since then, it and scores of other Bible societies have distributed millions of copies of the Bible around the world in all the main languages of the world. It was partly thanks to Mary Jones that the task of making the Bible available to all people began.

Look it Up

Christians believe that God took human form to live on earth as Jesus.

12 Christian Beliefs

Christians believe that, on the day Jesus was born, God became human. As they sometimes say, 'In Jesus, God was made flesh.' This is sometimes called the Incarnation (the word 'incarnate' means 'made flesh'). Another way of saying this is to say Jesus was 'God incarnate' – meaning Jesus was 'God made flesh'.

Christians also believe that, through his life, Jesus took the side of those

- who suffer
- who are 'done down' by more powerful people
- who are poor.

When Jesus suffered and died on the cross, he did it for these people. And by suffering and dying, Jesus took on himself the punishment for the wrongdoings of all those who believe in God.

Most importantly, Christians believe that by rising from the dead and being taken back into heaven, Jesus showed that he was indeed the Son of God and also that there was a new life after death.

Pentecost came after the end of Jesus' life on earth. Christians believe that on Pentecost God sent his Holy Spirit to be with (and to strengthen) those who believe.

So the most important Christian belief is that God has shown himself in three ways:

- God the Father, who is in heaven
- God the Son, who is God made human in the person of Jesus
- God the Holy Spirit, who continues to be present in this world.

Because of this, God is sometimes spoken of as being 'three in one' or the Holy Trinity. That does not mean there are three Christian 'Gods' but that the one God has three different forms.

In this fifteenth-century French painting, the artist Jean Fouquet has shown how he imagines the Trinity in heaven.

Trinity Sunday

Trinity Sunday celebrates the three ways that God has shown or 'manifested' himself. It is observed by many Christians on the Sunday after Pentecost because, with the coming of the Holy Spirit to the first apostles on that day, all three manifestations of God had then taken place.

The festival was first observed around the year 800 CE, especially in Germany, France and England. In Ireland, the three-leafed shamrock became a national emblem because, it was said, St Patrick (who first preached Christianity there) used the plant to teach about the Trinity.

Trinity Sunday is not observed by some Protestants and members of the Orthodox Church.

Creeds

These Christian beliefs are summed up in short statements known as 'creeds'. The word comes from the Latin *credo* which means 'I believe'.

This creed is known as the Apostles' Creed. It was probably written in the fourth century and is divided into three sections – about God the Father, God the Son and God the Holy Spirit.

I believe in God, the Father almighty,
creator of heaven and earth.

I believe in Jesus Christ, his only Son, our Lord,
who was conceived by the Holy Spirit,
born of the Virgin Mary,
suffered under Pontius Pilate,
was crucified, died, and was buried;
he descended to the dead.
On the third day he rose again;
he ascended into heaven,
he is seated at the right hand of the Father,
and he will come to judge the living and the dead.

I believe in the Holy Spirit,
the holy catholic• Church,
the communion of saints,
the forgiveness of sins,
the resurrection of the body,
and the life everlasting. Amen.
• 'catholic' here means 'universal'

Creeds are repeated by Christians during baptisms and other services as a way of stating publicly what they believe. Some Christians have written other statements of their faith to show their own slightly different beliefs.

Another form of this creed appears in a letter written by St Ambrose, around 390, but the creed may be even older.

Faith in God

When Christians say they believe in God, what does that mean?

Some people may simply mean 'I hope there is a God.'

Some Christians may mean 'I know there is a God.' They feel able to say this because they feel they have experienced the love and help of God in their lives and are certain that God is real.

Other Christians may mean 'I trust there is a God.' They cannot prove that God is real but they feel from what they see and sense and learn that there must be a God and are prepared to live their lives trusting in God.

St Ambrose's own writings provide one ancient version of a creed. Here, an Italian artist, Gasparo Diziani, imagines his joy on being in heaven.

Look it Up

4 The First Christmas
6 The Death and Resurrection of Jesus
7 The First Christians

Life was full of danger for the early Christians in the Roman empire.

Secret Meetings

To avoid being persecuted by the Roman authorities, Christians had to keep out of their way. This meant they had to meet and worship in secret. In Rome they did this in the many underground passageways and burial places that had been built under the city. These burial places were known as the catacombs.

The early Christians used secret signs carved on the walls to show each other the way to their meeting places. One sign was an outline carving of a fish. The Greek word for fish is *ichthus*. For Christians this was like a secret code – the letters of the Greek word spelling out their main belief:

IESOUS	Jesus
CHRISTOS	Christ
THEOU	God's
H**U**IOS	Son
SOTER	the Saviour

Look it Up

13 The Persecuted Church

As the number of people following the teachings of Jesus began to increase, they suffered attacks not only from the Jews but from the Romans. This was often because the Romans were suspicious of this new group of people but also because the Christians would not worship the Roman gods such as Mars the god of war and Apollo the sun god – as was required by Roman law.

As a result, there were times when the Roman rulers acted against Christians with great cruelty. Some Christians were put to death by crucifixion. Others were fed to captive lions. One of these was Bishop Polycarp (see Dying for the Faith on the right).

Even for 'ordinary' Christians, holding to the faith meant meeting in secret and risking death when spreading the 'good news' or Gospel of Jesus. Despite this, by the year 100 CE, there were Christians in many of the towns and cities around the eastern end of the Mediterranean Sea, as well as in Italy.

But matters became very much worse for Christians in the year 249. In that year, Decius became ruler of the Roman empire. He not only wanted everyone to worship the old gods of Rome but issued an order that everyone (throughout the whole empire) must offer a sacrifice to an image of the emperor. That is, they must worship Emperor Decius.

If people did that, they were given a letter proving their obedience. If they refused, as most Christians did, they risked being put to death.

Even so, Christians began to teach the Gospel in distant parts of the Roman empire which (by the year 300) stretched from Spain in the west to Jerusalem in the east, northwards to include England and south to the North African coast.

By this time there were four great centres of Christianity: Jerusalem, Antioch, Rome and the city which later became known as Constantinople.

Early Christians were killed by lions – to entertain the crowds in the Colosseum in Rome. A huge open-air arena, it is now a ruin.

Dying for the Faith

About the year 155, the Romans in the city of Smyrna in Asia Minor decided the Christians there were bringing bad luck to the city. The Christians' leader or bishop was an old man called Polycarp. He was taken to the local Roman governor who tried to persuade him to give up his faith. 'Just say it's all nonsense and make a sacrifice to the Roman gods.'

Polycarp refused. 'That would be saying what is true is untrue.' The governor threatened to throw him to the lions but Polycarp still refused to deny his belief in Jesus Christ. The governor then threatened he would put Polycarp to death by fire: he would be tied to a wooden stake and burned. Polycarp still didn't change his mind.

Polycarp was tied to the stake in front of a huge crowd. Soldiers set fire to the wood but the flames didn't seem to harm the old man. The governor finally ordered one of the soldiers to stab Bishop Polycarp one of many early Christians who were prepared to die rather than to give up their faith.

Agnes is often pictured with a lamb – simply because her name sounds like *agnus*, Latin for lamb.

St Agnes

Agnes was beautiful, clever and wealthy. She was thirteen, she lived in Rome and many men wanted to marry her but Agnes wanted to spend her life working for the Christian faith.

One of the young men who had fallen in love with her was the son of the city governor. When she rejected him, the governor sent for her and tried to persuade her to marry his son. Agnes refused.

'In that case,' he said, 'you must worship the Roman gods.' Again, Agnes refused to do what he said. 'In that case,' said the governor, 'you will be burned alive.' But when she was tied to a post and a fire was lit underneath her, she prayed aloud. The fire went out – and Agnes was eventually killed by a sword. All this happened in the year 304.

14 The Church and the Empire

For nearly 300 years following the death of Jesus, there were few Christians outside the Roman empire. Inside the Roman empire it was often dangerous to be known to be a Christian – because the Romans often persecuted Christians.

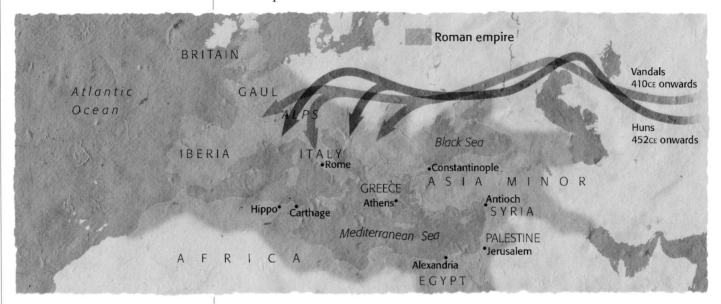

Roman empire

BRITAIN

Atlantic Ocean

GAUL

ALPS

Vandals 410CE onwards

Huns 452CE onwards

Black Sea

IBERIA

ITALY
•Rome

•Constantinople

ASIA MINOR

GREECE
Athens•

Antioch
•SYRIA

Hippo• Carthage

Mediterranean Sea

PALESTINE
•Jerusalem

AFRICA

Alexandria
EGYPT

The sign or 'cross' that Constantine had placed on his army's standards is called the chi-rho. The chi (X) and rho (P) that make up the sign are two Greek letters - the first two letters of the word Christ when written in Greek.

Look it Up

29 The Clergy of the Church
38 Saints of the Christian Church
(Both Constantine and John Chrysostom are honoured by Catholic Christians as saints.)

In the year 306, a man called Constantine had been named Emperor of Rome. At first, other Roman leaders did not recognize him as emperor. Then, in the year 312, he faced one of his rivals in battle. The night before that battle, Constantine believed Jesus appeared to him in a dream saying he must use the Christian cross as his own symbol and have it placed on his army's flags (or 'standards'). Constantine and his army won the battle easily.

As a result of his victory, Constantine made it legal for people in his empire to be Christian. A few years later (in 321), he made Sunday a public holiday so Christians could worship on that day. He also rebuilt the city of Byzantium in what is now Turkey to be his new capital city, instead of Rome. It became known as Constantinople. (It is now called Istanbul.) Constantine himself became a Christian and was baptized just before his death in 337.

Because Constantine (who became known as Constantine the Great) had made it legal to be a Christian, Christians could now build their own meeting places: churches. Constantine divided the empire into areas known as dioceses, each one looked after by a Christian leader known as a bishop.

The Church in Antioch

One centre of the faith was Antioch in Syria. In 381, a man known as John Chrysostom went to that city, later becoming its bishop. *Chrysostom* is a Greek word meaning 'Golden Mouth'. It was a nickname which he earned because his preaching so impressed his listeners. He was never afraid to say what he thought. Sometimes this meant he was quite tactless and upset people but he was always a friend of sinners. 'If you have done wrong not once but twice or even a thousand times, come to me. You will be healed, through Jesus Christ,' he said. And thousands of people did exactly that. Indeed, it is said that there were one hundred thousand Christians in Antioch when John was bishop.

John Chrysostom wrote many prayers. One is often said by Christians when they meet together in church. This is a modern version of part of that prayer:

'Almighty God… you promised that when two or three meet together in your Name, you will answer their prayers. Answer now, O Lord, the desires and requests of us, your servants, as may be best for us, granting us in this world knowledge of your word and in the world to come life everlasting, Amen.'

A nineteenth-century painting of John Chrysostom preaching.

By the end of that century, Christianity was the official religion of the Roman empire – from the Spanish coast in the west to Asia Minor in the east and from the African coast north to what is now England. After Constantine's death in the year 410, tribes from Asia (known as the Vandals) moved through Northern Europe and then south to capture Rome. Then, in 452, another tribe (called the Huns) also invaded from Asia hoping to capture Rome. The Bishop of Rome, Leo the Great, rode 200 miles on horseback to meet the leader of the Huns, Attila. Leo succeeded in persuading the Huns to turn back.

From now on, whoever was Bishop of Rome (or Pope) was a powerful and important leader. Some popes of this time began claiming to be the leader of all Christians.

15 The Expanding Church

Pope Gregory (who was pope from 590 to 604) told Augustine that he should 'Destroy as few pagan temples as possible… sprinkle them with holy water, (and) build altars.' When people in northern Europe became Christian, they did not completely forget their old religion at once. This stone shows both Christian crosses and the hammer-shaped badge of Thor.

St Boniface: Apostle of Germany

Boniface was born in the west of England in about 680 CE. He became a monk and journeyed to northern Europe to preach the Christian faith. Eventually he reached a town called Geismar in eastern Germany. On a nearby mountain grew a sturdy oak believed to be sacred to the pagan Norse god, Thor.

To prove Thor did not exist, Boniface said he would fell the tree. Believing Thor would strike him dead if he did, the townsfolk came to watch. Boniface cut the tree down without being harmed and the area became Christian.

An illustration from an eleventh-century service book showing moments from the life of Boniface.

Once the Romans had accepted the Christian faith, it spread throughout the empire and then slowly beyond the empire to the rest of Europe: to Russia, Scandinavia, Germany and Hungary. By the end of the first millennium (the first thousand years of Christianity), the religion dominated Europe and the Christian Church had spread the teachings of Jesus to the tribes that the Romans once called Vandals and Barbarians.

At the same time, however, followers of the Prophet Muhammad (known as Muslims) had begun to spread their religion west from the Prophet's homeland in Arabia. North Africa became Muslim instead of Christian – and there was conflict for control of Jerusalem.

The Crusades

Jerusalem has always been important to Christians because it was there that Jesus died on the cross and there that his resurrection took place. It is also a very holy place for Jews because it was there that the great Jewish Temple was built – and it had also become holy for Muslims. The Muslim religion, known as Islam, began in the year 610.

Soon after that, in 638, Jerusalem was captured by Muslims. This displeased both Christians and Jews. Much later, in November 1095, Pope Urban II called for Christians from all over Europe to win the city back for Christianity. This began a period of 'holy wars', known as the Crusades, that lasted for 200 years.

The First Crusade ended in the year 1099 when Christian armies recaptured the city. Some historians say the Christians killed 70,000 people during this attack. Muslims once again recaptured the city in 1187. Their leader Salah-ad-Din (some times known as Saladin) ordered that no Christian should be harmed and made peace with King Richard I of England, but there were yet more western crusades in later years.

Although Jesus taught his followers to make peace, not war, Christians at the time thought they were doing God's will. The Crusades are an unhappy part of the Christian story.

Christianity Reaches England

Pope Gregory once walked through Rome's market place. He saw a slave master selling young male slaves. Unlike most Roman slaves (who came from north Africa) they were blond and fair skinned. He was told they were Angles. 'They look more like angels,' he replied. 'Where are they from?'

'From Deira,' he was told.

'Then they must be rescued "De [from] ira",' answered Gregory, making a joke, because, although Deira was the name of part of the island where the Angles lived (now called England), the Latin words *Dei ira* also mean 'the anger of God'.

As a result, in the year 597, he sent a monk called Augustine to teach the Angles (or English) about Christianity. Augustine landed in Kent where the local king gave Augustine a palace in the city of Canterbury. Canterbury Cathedral was later built here.

This fifteenth-century miniature by Jean de Courcy shows Christians looting Jerusalem after they took the city – a far from Christian action.

Look it Up

14 The Church and the Empire
52 Christianity and Other Faiths

16 The Orthodox Churches

Icons

Both Greek and Russian Orthodox Christians give special honour to holy paintings known as icons (or 'images'). Painted on wood, they show Jesus or Mary or one of the other saints. They are not meant to be realistic (like photographs) but are meant to show the holiness and importance of the person they represent. They are sometimes called 'windows to heaven'.

An early icon of Jesus, dating from either the sixth or seventh century CE.

Constantine, the emperor who made Christianity the official religion of the Roman empire, moved its capital to the eastern city he named Constantinople. In the following years, the Christian faith spread northwards, reaching countries such as England and Germany.

But five cities around the Mediterranean Sea remained the great centres of Christianity. They were: Rome, where the pope was leader of the whole Church; Jerusalem; Alexandria in what is now Egypt; Antioch; and Constantinople (see map opposite).

Constantinople grew in wealth and importance. Rome, meanwhile, was weakened by Viking invasions from the north and by several quarrels about who should be pope. As a result, several popes were poisoned, strangled or put to death in other ways.

Rome and the eastern churches argued about other things. For example, the pope in Rome ordered the destruction of many icons (see left), saying they were like idols or false gods.

The great church of Hagia Sophia (meaning 'Holy Wisdom') is in Constantinople. It was built in just six years, being completed in 537.

Look it Up

14 The Church and the Empire
15 The Expanding Church
35 Inside an Orthodox Church

There were other rows. For example, should priests be allowed to marry? Should they have beards or not? The biggest argument was about whether the pope (living in Rome) should be leader of the whole Christian Church.

Eventually, the disagreements became too great. In 1054, the Church split in two. Such a break-up is called a schism. This split became known as the Great Schism. Matters became worse when the Crusaders came east. Many of them passed through Constantinople where they stole, destroyed icons and tore jewels from the cathedral altar.

Over the years, the western church became known as the Catholic (or Roman Catholic) Church; the various other eastern Churches (and also the Christian Church in Russia) became known as Orthodox Churches. Now they are known as the Russian, Greek and Armenian Orthodox Churches. Each uses its own language but their church services are similar. Unlike the Catholic Church, the Orthodox Churches do not have one overall leader.

Both Catholic and Orthodox Christians still teach the importance of the Bible; both have priests and bishops and observe saints' days (though not always on the same dates).

'Orthodox' means 'true' or 'right' while 'Catholic' means 'universal' or 'worldwide'.

The distribution of the Orthodox Churches after 1054.

The Coptic Church

The Christian Church in Egypt is known as the Coptic Church and dates back to the early days of Christianity. Some say it was started in Alexandria by St Mark (whose name is given to one of the four Gospels). Quarrels with most of the other Churches about whether Jesus was a human being as well as being the Son of God separated it from the other eastern Churches.

Nowadays, there are said to be between two and five million Copts, and their church services are in Arabic. Copts also run Sunday schools to teach the faith to their children and have restored some of the ancient desert monasteries – like this one in the Sinai Desert below, which was first built between 527 and 565.

Roman Catholics make up the largest group of Christians around the world.

Church Latin

All Roman Catholic church services, prayer books and even the Bible used were once in Latin, the language the Church had used since the time of the Roman empire. This meant that, wherever a Catholic went to church around the world, the service sounded more or less the same. The problem was that few Catholics understood Latin.

After many years, in 1965, Roman Catholic services were said in each country's own language. Even so, many Latin words once used in Catholic services are still known to many Christians. For example, a prayer which begins 'Hail Mary' is still known by those words in Latin, 'Ave Maria'.

Look it Up

14 The Church and the Empire
16 The Orthodox Churches
19 The Reformation
32 Christian Art

38

17 The Roman Catholic Church

Vatican City

Basilica of St Peter

St Peter's Square is a vast circular space which can hold 400,000 visitors or pilgrims.

Following the schism in the Church in the year 1054 CE, the western church based on Rome became known as the Catholic (or Roman Catholic) Church. The word 'catholic' means universal.

The apostle Peter is said to have been the first leader or bishop of the Christians in Rome. Each Bishop of Rome since then has been known as the pope. Catholics call this link back to Peter the 'apostolic succession'.

When the Roman empire became Christian, Emperor Constantine ordered a basilica to be built on the spot where Peter was thought to be buried. (A basilica is an important church which has a domed roof.) Much later, this was replaced by a new large church, St Peter's, built in the shape of a cross. The rebuilding began in 1506 and was completed in 1626.

St Peter's is part of the Vatican (the word comes from the Latin *Vaticanus*, the name of a hill in Rome). Since 1377, the Vatican has been the headquarters of the Roman Catholic Church and home of the pope. It is also a city and an independent country in the middle of Rome, the capital of Italy. Besides St Peter's Church, Vatican City includes the pope's palace, a separate chapel known as the Sistine Chapel, museums, a library and gardens. In modern times, a railway station, post office, radio and television stations and a supermarket have been added – but there are no hotels, restaurants or schools.

The pope is 'father' to millions of Roman Catholics who follow not only the teaching of the Bible but also that of their Church.

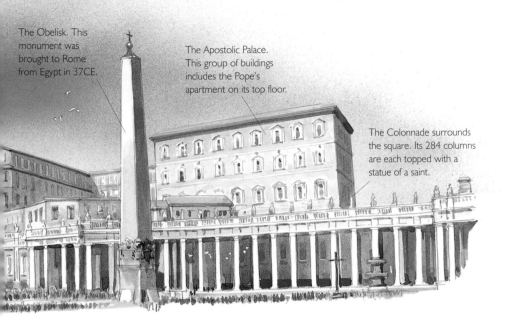

The Obelisk. This monument was brought to Rome from Egypt in 37CE.

The Apostolic Palace. This group of buildings includes the Pope's apartment on its top floor.

The Colonnade surrounds the square. Its 284 columns are each topped with a statue of a saint.

The Catholic Church Today

Half of the Christians in the world today are members of Roman Catholic Church. They are spread across all five continents but there are especially large numbers of Catholics in southern Europe, the United States of America, the Philippines and Central and South America. Indeed, half the Roman Catholics live in Central and South America.

Catholics are linked by their faith in Jesus and the leadership and the authority of the pope.

Pope Benedict XVI celebrates Mass (or Holy Communion) for young Catholics in Cologne, Germany.

The Papacy

The job or authority of being pope is known as the Papacy. Over the centuries, following the schism of 1054, the Papacy became very powerful in western Europe – and the pope was able to tell kings and queens how they should rule. He even 'excommunicated' some kings which meant they were forbidden to receive holy communion or to be part of the Church.

One pope (Innocent III, who lived from 1161 to 1216) created new schools, monasteries and convents. He persuaded the bishops to make sure their priests were better educated. Each cathedral was to have a school and a hospital. Many great new churches were built and beautifully decorated.

Over these years, the Catholic Church did much good but, by the sixteenth century, many people thought it was getting too powerful, too rich and too greedy. Some people began to think it should be reformed.

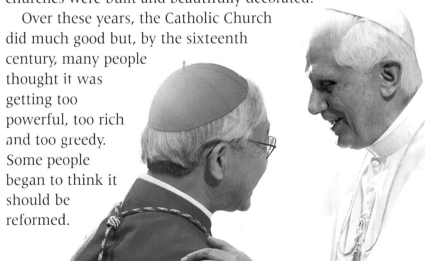

Pope Benedict XVI greets a cardinal from Hong Kong.

Roman Catholics respect the teachings of Jesus and the authority of their Church in different ways.

This nun works as a teacher in India.

18 Living for Christ

Monks and nuns are men and women who have chosen to devote their whole lives to God. They usually make three vows:

• The vow of poverty (to own nothing of their own)
• The vow of chastity (to have no sexual relations)
• The vow of obedience (to obey the will of God and the rules of the group or 'order' of monks or nuns to which they belong).

In the first centuries of the Christian Church, some men and women lived like hermits, often on their own and often in desert places. They lived with little sleep and often fasted.

Many monks and nuns also choose to live apart from the world but in groups or 'orders' – in buildings called either monasteries or convents. They spend their time in prayer and Bible study and may go to as many as seven church services a day.

One order of monks became known as the Benedictines, after the man who started the order, Benedict (480–550 CE). Benedict wrote a 'Rule' or way of life for his followers. He didn't want to make life too strict for his monks in case they got discouraged when they failed to keep it. Nor did he want to make life too easy.

His Rule said that his fellow monks should meet in church several times a day to pray and to listen to Bible readings. But he said it was just as important that the monks should work. They should grow all their own food, prepare their own meals, mend the monastery when necessary and copy books in beautiful handwriting. He said, 'To work is to pray.' He also believed that idleness is 'the enemy of the soul'. His Rule is still followed by Benedictine communities all around the world.

These Franciscan friars are walking in procession to church in Jerusalem on Easter Sunday.

Look it Up

A famous painting by the Italian artist Giotto shows Francis giving away his possessions – including his own clothes.

St Francis

A rich young Italian called Francis Bernardone (around 1181–1226) used to spend his time going to parties and enjoying life. After an illness, he spent more time praying and became certain God wanted him to help the poor.

He gave away his possessions and started to live a simple life. Other young men joined him and they became known as Franciscans, after their leader. They moved from place to place, in a group, helping the poor, comforting those who were ill or dying and greeting everyone with the words, 'The peace of God be with you.' Although their life was a little like that of monks, they were properly called 'friars' (or brothers).

When there were too many of them to live in one group, Francis wrote down a 'Rule' for their way of life. They were to promise to live in poverty and to have no possessions, not to marry nor to have any kind of love life, and to be obedient at all times. This 'Rule' was later approved by the pope. Present-day followers of St Francis still live by the same Rule.

St Clare

In the year 1207, soon after Francis had given up all his wealth to live a life of simple poverty, he met a young woman called Clare (1194–1253). Gradually she too decided she wanted to serve Jesus through poverty. At first, Clare lived in a nearby Benedictine convent but soon other women followed her example of living a very simple life. They never ate meat, they did without shoes and stockings, and had no personal property. Eventually, they became a separate group or 'order' of nuns, a sister order to the Franciscans, and are still known as the Poor Clares.

A member of the Poor Clares reads her Bible beside her simple bed.

Other orders of monks and nuns also work, perhaps by gardening or making things to sell in order to pay for the things their monastery or convent needs. In modern times, more and more monks and nuns have begun to live in the ordinary world, keeping their vows but working as teachers, nurses or doing other work.

There are also monks and nuns in the Orthodox and Anglican Churches.

Erasmus

Desiderius Erasmus was a Dutch Christian who lived from about 1466 until 1536. A wise and witty man, he wrote many books that made fun of the Church's weaknesses. He studied Hebrew and Greek (the languages the Bible was originally written in) so he could understand it better. He also hated violence.

He wanted the Catholic Church to reform itself. Instead, he inspired other people to create new churches. Chief among these reformers was someone called Martin Luther.

Look it Up

20 The Protestant Churches
23 Missions to the World
34 Holy Communion
46 Death: in Sure and Certain Hope

19 The Reformation

By the early 1500s, there was much wrong with the Church in western Europe. In some places, the local church leaders or priests could not even read or write. The Church made money by selling the best jobs (such as being a bishop) to those who paid the most, even if they were not suitable for the job.

The Church was also trying to make money by selling 'indulgences'. People called pardoners journeyed around Europe selling these worthless pieces of paper, said to have come from the pope. If you bought one, the pardoner promised your sins would be forgiven and you would go to heaven. You could also buy indulgences that were supposed to save your dead relatives from hell or purgatory.

Many ordinary people were fooled by the pardoners and handed over their money.

At the same time, some of the kings and princes who ruled the different countries in Europe were getting tired of being told what to do by the pope. And with the invention of printing around this time, books (including the Bible) were becoming available to people other than priests. New ideas began to spread quickly. Soon, talk of protest and of reforming the Church began to spread from country to country.

In some places, those who felt it was too difficult to change the Catholic Church started new, independent Churches. This happened especially in the northern half of Europe. These 'protest' Churches became known as the Protestant Churches and included the Lutherans in Germany and Scandinavia, the Calvinists and the Presbyterians.

This woodcut, created about 1524, illustrates the corrupt trade in indulgences.

Ignatius Loyola, founder of the Jesuits.

The Catholic Reformation

As new Churches were formed, the Church in Rome began to reform itself. It opened new schools, began new missionary work in America and East Asia, and made its church services more dignified. New 'orders' of priests were also started.

A man called Ignatius who came from Loyola in Spain was joined by a group of friends. They felt they were an army of soldiers fighting for Jesus and took the name Society of Jesus. They are often known as Jesuits.

Two Bible Translators

John Wycliffe (1320–84) lived long before Luther and was one of the first to speak of the need for reform. He became very critical of the bishops for never having allowed the Bible to be translated into English – a task which he undertook with the help of others.

William Tyndale (1494–1536) went to Germany, met Luther, and there translated the New Testament into English. It was printed in 1526. He started work on the Old Testament but was pursued by secret agents, caught and burned to death.

During the Reformation, many Protestants were burned to death by their Catholic enemies.

Religious Wars

Between the start of the Reformation and its end (in 1648), the many disagreements between Catholics and Protestants led not only to bitter quarrels but to bloody battles and fierce wars. Thousands lost their lives as Catholic and Protestant countries fought each other.

A Roman Catholic system of courts called the Inquisition hunted out men and women whom it claimed held false beliefs. Held in secret, these trials led to many being tortured, flogged, imprisoned or burned to death. Some were even put to death by being boiled in oil. In Protestant countries, Catholics were forced to meet in secret. If they were caught, they were put on trial and often sentenced to death.

Different 'protesting' or Protestant Churches developed in different European countries.

Luther's Conversion

As Luther studied the Bible, he realized something many Christians of that time had forgotten. The message of Jesus is about love and forgiveness; not punishment for wrongdoing. 'When I realized this,' he said, 'I felt born again!' He was remembering some words of Jesus: 'No one can see the Kingdom of God without being born again.' (John 3:3).

Martin Luther nails his ninety-five 'theses' to the door of Wittenberg Cathedral.

Look it Up

44

20 The Protestant Churches

Before the Reformation, many parishes had been left without priests. Monks and nuns had forgotten their vows of poverty and lived in luxury. Bishops kept the best jobs for their friends. Men like Martin Luther began to protest. These protests led to them being called Protestants.

Martin Luther was born in 1483. He became a monk, then a priest – and then a university lecturer at Wittenberg, in what is now Germany. In 1510, he visited Rome. He was shocked at the wealth of the churchmen there and the way they lived.

Back in Germany, he felt the Bible was more important than any churchman. He said that the Bible should be available to everyone, in their own language and not just in Latin – just as men like Wycliffe and Tyndale had said.

He made his views known in the usual way for those days. He wrote out what he believed and then nailed the papers to the church door so everyone could read them. They became known as his *Ninety-Five Theses* (or 'statements').

This map shows the spread of Protestantism and the distribution of religions in Europe at the end of the Reformation.

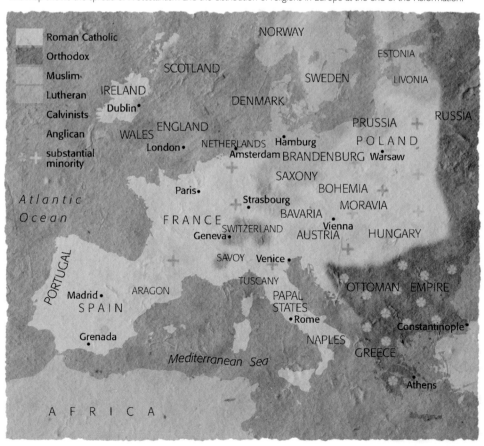

Three Great Reformers

Ulrich Zwingli (1484–1531)

Ulrich Zwingli became a priest at a church in Zurich in Switzerland and attacked many Catholic customs. He was against fasting in Lent, monks and nuns, indulgences, praying to the saints and respecting the pope. He wanted there to be no crucifixes, statues or richly decorated curtains in churches – and for there to be no organ music or chanting.

John Calvin (1509–64)

John Calvin (who was French) disagreed with the authority of the pope and the bishops and with most of the Catholic festivals. He rejected the importance of Jesus' mother, Mary. What mattered most, he said, was the teachings of the Bible, but he did believe that Jesus was, in some way, present at Holy Communion. Like Luther, he believed that faith was what earned you a place in heaven. Calvinists now believe that God has chosen some people to be saved in heaven and not others.

John Knox (around 1513–72)

Originally a Catholic priest, Knox preached in favour of the Reformation and had to flee his native Scotland to live in France and later Switzerland. He studied under Calvin. He returned to become a leader of the Scottish Protestants. After several years of bloody fighting between Catholics and Protestants, the state church of Scotland became Presbyterian. Each group of its members is looked after by a minister or presbyter (meaning 'overseer'). The Presbyterian Church has spread to every continent and its beliefs are similar to those of Calvinists.

Some people said Luther should be burned as a heretic (a person who doesn't believe the things the church officially teaches), but a friendly German prince kept Luther safely inside his castle. There, Luther translated the Bible into German.

When the pope published a statement saying Luther was wrong, Luther burned that statement in public. The pope then 'excommunicated' him – that is, stopped him being a member of the Church. Luther refused to change his mind and made this declaration: 'Here I stand, I can do no other.'

Luther never meant to break with the Roman Catholic Church. He wanted to reform it. But many people started new 'Lutheran' churches. These spread from Germany to Denmark and to what are now Norway, Sweden and Finland.

Their buildings were plainer than the Catholic ones of that time. For example, they contained no pictures of the saints. Lutherans said all honour should be given to Jesus alone.

This light and airy Lutheran church in Reykjavik, Iceland, contrasts with the ornate pre-Reformation Catholic Churches.

After the Reformation, many Christians started 'breakaway' Churches – sometimes called 'denominations'.

21 Differing Denominations

Although the Roman and the Orthodox Churches separated almost a thousand years ago, they still teach similar things and their church services are built on the same idea: the sacrifice of Jesus on the cross happens again in each Holy Communion – whether it is called the Mass or Eucharist.

Protestant church services can look very different. In many of them, what is most important is 'the Word', the teachings of the Bible.

The Anglican Communion

In England, it was not a religious leader like Martin Luther or John Knox who brought about the reform of the Church. It was the king, Henry VIII – who had earlier attacked all that Luther had been teaching.

Henry wanted to divorce his first wife and marry another woman called Anne Boleyn. The pope would not agree. Henry's chief archbishop, a man called Thomas Cranmer, eventually said Henry's marriage could be 'annulled' (which means 'made nothing'). This led to a row between England and Rome. Henry was named head of the Church of England – and married Anne. Even so, he kept the traditional services of the Catholic Church and (at first) burned those who 'dared' to translate the Bible into English.

Meanwhile, Thomas Cranmer gradually introduced Protestant ideas into the Church of England and, after Henry died, produced a book of new church services called *The Book of Common Prayer*. It is still in use in some churches.

The Church of England still claims to be both Catholic and Protestant. In more recent times, 'sister churches' have been started, especially in other English-speaking countries such as Australia, Canada and some African countries. In America there is the Episcopalian Church of the USA. Together these Churches form the Anglican Communion.

King Henry VIII of England declared his Church to be free of papal authority. This painting of him is by Hans Holbein.

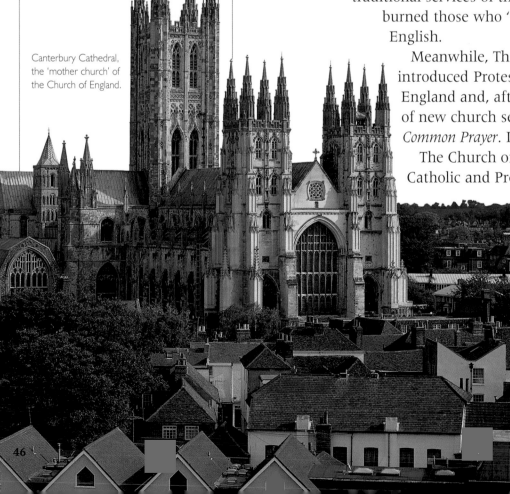

Canterbury Cathedral, the 'mother church' of the Church of England.

The Baptists

One of the many different groups of Protestants in Europe became known as the Baptists. Their belief was that people should be baptized only when they were old enough to decide for themselves that this was what they wanted. Baptist Churches soon spread:

- 1609 The Netherlands
- 1612 England
- 1639 America.

The Methodists

Born in 1703, young John Wesley had a lucky escape when he was just six. The house where he lived caught fire. Farm workers managed to rescue him before the house was destroyed. His mother said he was 'a brand snatched from the burning'. He never forgot this and knew he had been saved to do some special work.

In 1735, he went to America with his brother Charles to teach Native Americans about Christianity. He did much good but knew he still hadn't found the special work he was meant to be doing – so he returned to England.

One night, at a Moravian meeting in London, someone read from the works of Martin Luther. Wesley later said, 'I felt my heart strangely warmed. I felt I did trust in Christ.'

Within a few months, John Wesley had started preaching his message that God loves everyone who believes in him and that heaven is waiting for all believers. He preached in the streets, in fields and at crossroads in the countryside. Other preachers copied him.

Wesley wrote rules or 'methods' for his followers. This led to them becoming known as Methodists and, from 1784 onwards, Methodism was a separate church.

The Society of Friends

When he was nineteen, a young Englishman called George Fox heard an 'inner voice' telling him to become a wandering preacher. He disliked organized Church of England services and sometimes interrupted them to preach his own beliefs. In about 1650, he started a 'Society of Friends'. He and his supporters went to many countries including North America, the West Indies and the Netherlands. Having spent six years in prison for preaching against the 'official' Church, he worked hard to improve prisons and was also a pacifist – being against all war. Members of the Society of Friends (often known as Quakers) continue this work and belief.

The First African Baptist Church in Savannah, Georgia, USA, established in 1773. The present building dates from 1859.

John Wesley, preaching in Cornwall, England.

Look it Up

Christianity arrived in North America thanks to early missionaries. Later, it developed and grew as Europeans settled across the continent.

22 North American Protestants

People argue who was the first European explorer to reach America but we know for certain that an Italian called Christopher Columbus (sailing on behalf of the King of Spain) reached the Caribbean in 1492. His expedition was followed by many more explorers from Spain and later Portugal. They were Roman Catholics and brought their faith with them as they explored what is now Central and South America. For this reason, most of the countries in this part of the world are still Roman Catholic.

Later, many Europeans decided to move to the Americas and to start a new life there. Many of those who settled in North America came from northern European countries. They included Roman Catholics but also Christians from the different Protestant Churches – some of whom moved to America because of opposition to their particular beliefs in their own European countries. One group from England was known as Puritans. They had wanted to 'purify' the Church of England of bishops and the special vestments worn by its priests. They also wanted to keep Sunday very holy.

Eventually, in 1620, a group of them crossed the Atlantic on the sailing ship *Mayflower* and landed at Plymouth, in New England, now called Massachusetts. They became known as the Pilgrim Fathers.

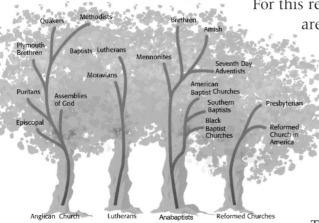

Quakers   Methodists   Brethren
Amish
Plymouth Brethren   Baptists   Lutherans   Mennonites
Seventh Day Adventists
Moravians
American Baptist Churches
Puritans   Assemblies of God   Southern Baptists   Presbyterian
Black Baptist Churches
Episcopal   Reformed Church in America

Anglican Church   Lutherans   Anabaptists   Reformed Churches

Anabaptists

The Anabaptists began as small groups of Protestants in Europe during the Reformation. Their name means 'baptized again' as they insisted that anyone baptized as a baby should be baptized again as an adult. They refused to go to war and this led them into conflict in several countries. Many of them moved to North America where they could live as they wished.

Some of the Anabaptist communities in North America still keep to the lifestyle they chose around the time of their founding.

Look it Up

Besides the main Protestant Churches, other smaller Churches have flourished in the United States of America. Among them are:

Mennonites

The Mennonites are a Protestant denomination which grew out of the Anabaptist movement. Groups of Mennonites exist in Germany, the Netherlands, Russia, North America and some other countries. All believe in adult baptism.

The Amish

This Church was begun in 1693 by a group of Mennonites. Most of them moved to America and now live in Pennsylvania. They are committed to a simple lifestyle and so they tend to live apart in their own communities without any modern technology.

Seventh Day Adventists

This Christian group or sect believes in adult baptism and keeps the seventh day of the week (Saturday) as the sabbath or holy day (in the same way that Jews do). They are also strongly against alcohol.

Moravians

The Moravians were originally Lutheran Christians. They believe firmly in the Bible as a guide to their daily living.

Great Awakenings

During the mid 1700s, when the Methodist Revival was happening in England, another Christian revival happened in what were then known as the American colonies. Many powerful preachers journeyed through the states. Some preachers simply frightened their listeners into becoming devout Christians by delivering sermons describing the horrors of hellfire. This movement later became known as the First Great Awakening.

A Second Great Awakening took place in the early years of the next century. This time, preachers offered salvation to those who 'made a new start' or were prepared to be 'born again'.

This 1971 re-enactment of the first Thanksgiving Dinner shows how the original Pilgrims blessed their food and gave thanks to God for the harvest.

Thanksgiving

When the Pilgrim Fathers arrived in America, a harsh winter claimed many lives. By the next summer, it was clear they would have a good harvest and the Pilgrims held a three-day celebration, feeding on turkeys, geese, ducks and deer.

During the American War of Independence (1775–83), General George Washington ordered eight days to be marked as days of thanksgiving for victories over the British. In 1863, President Abraham Lincoln ordered that the last Thursday in November should be a national day of Thanksgiving.

Thanksgiving now reflects multi-faith and secular aspects of American society as well as early co-operation between the Pilgrim Fathers and Native Americans. For most Americans, the main event is the family meal which contains many reminders of the early harvest thanksgivings: turkey, sweet potato, cranberry sauce and pumpkin pie.

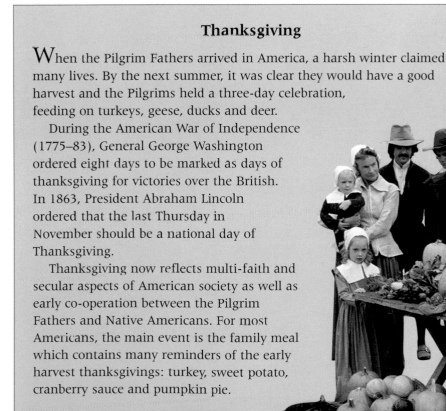

Christians believe it is important to spread the teachings of Jesus around the world.

Francis Xavier

Some missionaries journeyed eastwards from Europe. One of them was Francis Xavier. Although he was a Spaniard, he was sent by the King of Portugal and landed at Goa on the west coast of India in 1542. Francis helped people in hospital and prison there and, to his surprise, he found one group of Indian people who already followed Jesus. These people called themselves the Christians of St Thomas – believing their faith had been brought to them centuries earlier by the same Thomas who was one of Jesus' original twelve disciples.

During the next few years, Francis journeyed to the Malay Peninsula, where he heard stories about a country which no European had ever visited: Japan. Francis became the first European to reach Japan and there he converted at least two thousand people to Christianity.

Look it Up

23 Missions to the World

In the Gospel of St Matthew, we read what Jesus said to his disciples at the very end of his life on earth. 'Go, then, to all peoples everywhere and make them my disciples, baptize them… and teach them to obey everything that I have commanded you.' (Matthew 28:19–20.) At different times and in different ways, Christians have tried to follow this instruction by telling people who have never heard of Jesus all about him: about what he did and what he taught. Someone who does this work is called a 'missionary'. The word means someone who is sent out – to do a particular job.

There have been two great periods of missionary work when Christians have gone out from Europe to countries around the world.

The First World Missions

In the fifteenth and sixteenth centuries, Spanish explorers travelled to Mexico, Central America and South America. Portuguese explorers travelled to Brazil and to countries in Africa, India and East Asia. These explorers went in search of gold and to claim new lands to be ruled by the kings and queens of Spain and Portugal. Priests and monks travelled with them in order to teach the people they found there about Christianity.

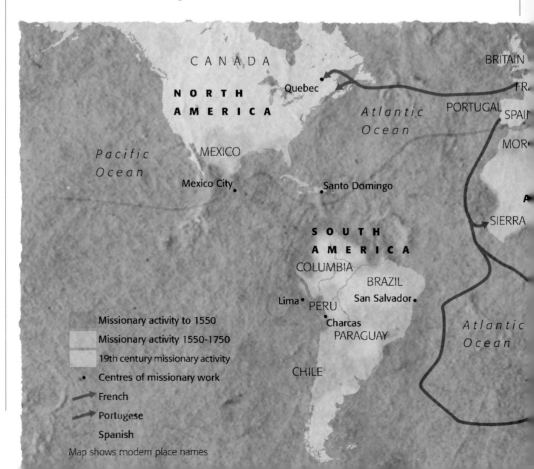

Missionary activity to 1550
Missionary activity 1550-1750
19th century missionary activity
Centres of missionary work
French
Portugese
Spanish
Map shows modern place names

The Christian missionaries who travelled to Mexico and Central America were very successful. By the year 1540, over eight million people had become Christians in Mexico. Because these missionaries came from Catholic countries, the people in Central and South America became Catholic Christians.

The Second Great Missionary Era

By 1800, ships from European countries were regularly visiting every part of the world. As people in Europe began to hear about different peoples in distant lands, many Christians decided to take the 'good news' or Gospel of Jesus Christ to those peoples. Another great period of missionary work began.

In countries such as Britain, France, Germany and Belgium, and also in North America, charities were formed to support and pay for this work. For example, the Church Missionary Society was started in England in 1799. In 1816, the American Bible Society was founded to provide Bibles for people who had come to live in America and could not afford them, for Native Americans and for people overseas.

Christian missionary work continues today – but sometimes it is done by missionaries from Africa and South America who come to Europe and North America to preach to non-Christians there.

Doctor Livingstone, I presume?

One famous missionary of the nineteenth century was a Scotsman called David Livingstone. The London Missionary Society sent him to work in South Africa. He spoke out against ill-treatment of black Africans by some white merchants who treated them as slaves. When Africans became Christians, he helped them to become missionaries to their own people.

Later, he journeyed to Central Africa to spread the Gospel there. For some time, nobody knew where he was and a New York journalist called Henry Morton Stanley set out to find him. Eventually he did, asking a question that became famous, 'Doctor Livingstone, I presume?'

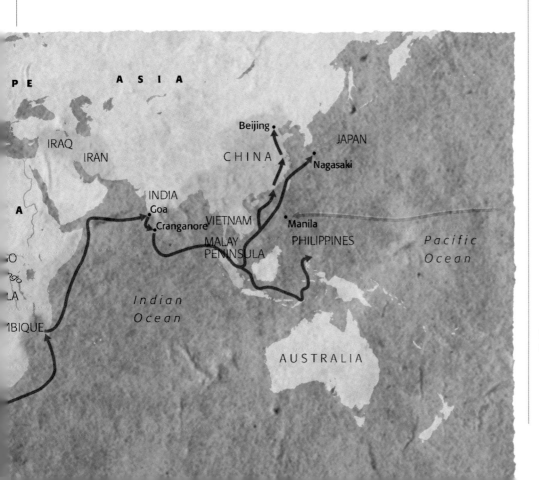

Routes taken by missionaries in the sixteenth and nineteenth centuries.

Despite being persecuted by Communists, the Christian churches still thrive in Russia.

'Father' Tikhon

At the time of the Russian Revolution, the Orthodox Church in that country was run by a group of bishops and other people. At a meeting, one of them stood up. 'We no longer have a Tsar. We need a patriarch.' ('Patriarch' is a name or title usually given to the head of a family.)

They chose a man called Tikhon who had been a monk but was now one of the bishops. Crowds came to see him made Patriarch in a cathedral inside what had been the Kremlin fortress in Moscow. It was almost the last church service to be held there for seventy years. Soon afterwards, Tikhon was arrested.

Look it Up

24 The Church in Russia

World War I began in 1914. Alongside all the terrible fighting, living conditions grew worse and worse in Russia. They were so bad that, in 1917, they helped spark a revolution in Russia. The ruler of Russia, the Tsar, and all his family, were murdered. The new rulers were Communists, led by a man called Lenin. Communists wanted to end the control held by privileged such as the Tsar, landowners and the Church.

Lenin believed religion (and especially the Russian Orthodox Church) acted like a drug that stopped Russia from becoming the sort of country he and his followers wanted it to be. He also thought the Orthodox Church was a rival power; one that he would have to destroy if Communism were to control the country.

Within just a few years of the Russian Revolution, more than one thousand bishops and priests had been executed. Hundreds of monasteries were destroyed. Church treasures were seized. The Communists attacked not only the Orthodox Church, they also stopped Jews and Muslims living in Russia from attending synagogues and mosques and made it a crime to teach children about God.

When Lenin died in 1924, his place was taken by another Communist, Joseph Stalin. He was even harsher. Many more clergy were put in prison. Lutheran, Baptist and Roman Catholic Christians living in Russia were also punished. It wasn't until 1988 that a new President, Mikhail Gorbachev, announced that 'mistakes have been made in such matters as religion'.

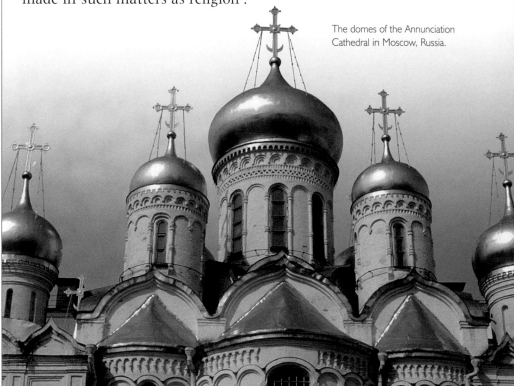

The domes of the Annunciation Cathedral in Moscow, Russia.

The next year Patriarch Tikhon was named a saint. A ceremony to mark this took place in the Cathedral in the Kremlin – the first service to be held there for seventy years. It was also almost exactly one thousand years after the Christian message first reached Russia.

This was the start of a new period of freedom and openness or *glasnost* for not only the Orthodox but other Churches in Russia. Millions of Bibles were handed out and the people once again felt free to go to church. About half of Russia's population of 150 million people are now thought to believe in Christianity.

In more recent years, the Russian Orthodox Church has again tried to become the 'official' religion of Russia and to ban Protestant Churches.

A screen covered in icons at Smolensk Cathedral, Moscow, Russia.

St Basil's Cathedral in Moscow, Russia.

The Russian Orthodox Church

500 years
- 500 CE onwards: Christianity spreads northwards from the Roman empire

- 863: Two brothers, Cyril and Methodius, take the faith to the Slavonic countries and use the Slavonic language in worship. Later, Churches in Bulgaria and Russia also begin using local languages

1000 years
- 988: Russia becomes officially Christian
- 1054: The Orthodox (eastern) Churches split from Rome

- 1453: The Russian Church becomes independent of Constantinople

1500 years
- 1500s, 1600s: The Orthodox Church becomes the centre of Russian life

- 1800s: Russian missionaries spread the Christian faith eastwards through Siberia and other parts of Asia, and eventually to China, Japan and even Alaska

- 1917: The Russian Revolution

- 1929–30 and 1937–38: Persecution of the Orthodox Church

- 1988: *Glasnost*: religion is again permitted

- 1988–93: One third of Russia's population under the age of 30 are openly Orthodox Christians

2000 years

THE CHURCH

The Christian Church is especially strong in this part of the world.

Protestant Growth

From the 1960s onwards, the number of Protestant Christians in Central and South America also began to increase. Many Pentecostal or charismatic Protestant churches were started and their numbers have quickly grown. Of the Christians in Central and South America, two thirds are Roman Catholic and the rest are Protestant. Of this third, three quarters are members of Pentecostal churches.

25 The Church in Central and South America

As soon as the first Spanish and Portuguese explorers reached Central and South America, missionaries began preaching the Christian message to the people they found there. As a result, many people in this part of the world became Roman Catholic Christians. During the Second Great Missionary Era (in the 1800s), when missionaries again began to travel the world in order to spread the Gospel, they concentrated on Africa and East Asia. South America was 'left to itself'. Not everything was well, however. Quarrels started between the Church and the governments of some of the countries. In one country, Paraguay, the president even made himself head of the Church. Many of these quarrels continued into the twentieth century as the Church and non-religious rulers struggled to influence the people. In one case (see right), it resulted in the murder of an archbishop.

At the same time (and partly because of these struggles), the number of Christians in Central and South America continued to grow. Because of these increasing numbers, the Roman Catholic leader, Pope John Paul II, made several visits to the continent.

Meanwhile, many of the people continued to live in great poverty. In 1968, a group of Central and Southern American bishops had a meeting and said that the poor people of their region must be helped. They encouraged the poor to work together and even to rebel in order to improve their own lives and so gain freedom from poverty. This teaching and action became known as 'Liberation Theology'.

Not everyone thought it a good thing. Some people (including some within the Roman Catholic Church) said that this teaching was more like Communism than Christianity. After a visit to Brazil, Pope John Paul said he did not agree completely with Liberation Theology but he did say how important was the fight against poverty.

Built on top of the Corcovado Mountain in Rio de Janeiro, Brazil, the huge statue of Christ the Redeemer shows Jesus stretching out his arms in protection and blessing of the city. One of the world's best-known and most-visited monuments, it illustrates the importance of the Christian faith in this part of the world.

The Murdered Archbishop

In 1980 El Salvador was the smallest and most densely populated country in Central America. It was under army rule. Death squads roamed the country. But also busy in El Salvador were men who called themselves 'freedom fighters'. Others called them terrorists. Suffering between the two warring groups were the people of El Salvador.

The country's archbishop was a man called Oscar Romero. One of his priests had been murdered by an army death squad. His death made Oscar Romero speak out – and he refused to attend any parades and ceremonies the army chiefs organized. They were not pleased.

Archbishop Romero went on speaking out on the side of the poor. He made lists of people who had 'disappeared' – which usually meant they'd been murdered. Not surprisingly, he became popular with the poor of El Salvador. His speeches gained attention abroad. The army-led government wanted him silenced.

One Monday evening, he was about to celebrate mass in a hospital chapel. As the archbishop stood at the altar, four men walked in and shot him dead – simply because he had dared to speak out against brutality.

A festival in honour of the Virgin Mary in Mexico attracts local people in traditional dress.

God and the Poor

In Central and South America – as in other places – Christians have struggled against the injustive of a few rich people exploiting the poor. They point to passages such as this, from the Old Testament prophet Amos:

'You have oppressed the poor and robbed them of their grain. And so you will not live in the fine stone houses you build or drink wine from the beautiful vineyards you plant… Make it your aim to do what is right, not what is evil, so that you may live. Then the Lord God Almighty really will be with you, as you claim he is. Hate what is evil, love what is right, and see that justice prevails in the courts.'

Amos 5:10–11, 14–15

Look it Up

17 The Roman Catholic Church
23 Missions to the World
28 The Pentecostal Movement
50 The Fight for Justic Continues

26 The Church in Africa

Christianity reached Africa in the time of the Roman empire. The Coptic Church in Egypt and the Ethiopian Church have survived to this day. But it was from about 1850 that Christian missionaries from Europe began to travel widely in Africa, taking the teachings of Jesus to those who lived there. In areas where the religion of Islam was strong they made few converts, but Christian churches were started in northern Africa (especially Algeria), western Africa, Uganda, the Congo region and South Africa.

Over the years, Africans such as Samuel Adjai Crowther became priests and ministers, but the African churches were still led by white men. It was only after World War I that the pope (Benedict XV) said that African clergy should become bishops. During the twentieth century, the number of Christians in Africa grew very rapidly from 10 million in 1900 to 100 million in 1980. By the year 2000 the number had certainly reached 200 million and may have been as high as 400 million.

Now almost half the population of Africa is Christian. In some countries (including the Central African Republic, Kenya and Lesotho) three quarters of the populations are Christian. The largest denomination is the Roman Catholic Church but 'local', independent Protestant Churches are also strong. Several were started by charismatic leaders, some of who were moved by experiencing visions – as Isaiah Shembe was.

Shembe

Isaiah Shembe was one of several African Church leaders who saw visions of Jesus. His Church, the Church of the Nazarites, which he founded in 1911, is often known simply as 'Shembe'. Its followers celebrate their faith by singing and dancing.

One of the great fighters against apartheid was Desmond Tutu, who became Archbishop of Cape Town in South Africa in 1986.

Look it Up

An outdoor church service, held in Namibia, south-west Africa.

**Set Free in Freetown:
Bishop Samuel Adjai
Crowther**

Adjai grew up in what is now Nigeria in west Africa. As a boy, he was kidnapped and sold to illegal 'slavers' who exported young Africans by ship to America to sell as slaves there. Luckily for Adjai, this slave ship was spotted by the British Navy.

Adjai (and the other slave boys on board) were set free in a port called Freetown in Sierra Leone in 1822. There he learned to read and write and became a Christian. Later he went to London to study but returned to Sierra Leone to teach. He went back to London to study to become a priest in 1843. On 29 June 1864, in Canterbury Cathedral, he became the first black African to be made an Anglican (or Episcopalian) bishop. It is thanks to him that Nigerians first heard about Jesus.

In its early years, the Christian Church in Europe adopted pagan festivals and made them Christian. Something similar happened in Africa as the religion spread through that continent. African churches adopted local customs related to witchcraft and ancestor worship. For example, a native custom of worshipping dead relatives is developing into a way of requesting relatives in heaven to pray for those on earth – just as some Christians ask the saints to pray for them.

African Christians are often strong in their faith and express it with great enthusiasm, keeping strictly to its teachings. Some are now working as missionaries in European countries.

But the story of the Church in Africa has not always been a happy one. During the 1970s, Uganda was ruled by a dictator called Idi Amin. Many Christians became his victims. When the leader of the Ugandan Church, Archbishop Janani Luwum, spoke out against Idi Amin, it was announced he had been killed in a car crash. In fact, he had been murdered.

Sometimes the troubles have been caused by Christians. In southern Africa, the Dutch Reformed Church supported the policy of keeping blacks and whites separate, known as apartheid. It led to much suffering and great hardship among the black population. Happily, many Christians also worked hard to end apartheid and bring about reconciliation.

Although Christianity is often described as a 'western' religion, it has many followers in Asia and Australasia.

• Korea was occupied by Japan from 1910 to 1945. During this time, many Koreans became Christian. Today, there are over 14 million Christians in the country.

One in five people who live in India is Christian.

An evangelical Church is now active in Vietnam. It has half a million members.

One in five people who live in Singapore is Christian.

Although Indonesia is mainly Muslim, ten per cent of the population is Christian.

27 The Church in East Asia and Australasia

The main religions of East Asia are Hinduism, Buddhism and Sikhism. The huge island country of Indonesia is mainly Muslim. For these reasons, it is easy to imagine that there are not many Christians in this part of the world. Indeed, in the Asian continent, only three or four out of every hundred people are Christian.

But the huge continent of Asia contains over half the world's population. As so many millions of people who live there, it means that, although Christians are only a small part of the population, there are still large numbers of them. In fact, one in ten of the world's Christians lives in Asia. The most active Christian Churches across the Asian continent are Roman Catholic and Pentecostal ones.

RUSSIA

CHINA

KOREA   JAPAN

INDIA

Pacific Ocean

VIETNAM

PHILIPPINES

SINGAPORE

Indian Ocean

INDONESIA

AUSTRALIA

- Francis Xavier was one of the first missionaries to reach China and Japan.
- From 1840 onwards, Christian missionaries began to spread the faith in China.
- In 1949, China became (like Russia) a Communist country. Ever since, the government has limited the work of missionaries and churches.

- Ever since Spain captured the Philippine islands during the 1500s, the Philippines has been a strongly Roman Catholic country.

Many islands in the South Pacific became Christian.

- Christianity came to countries which form Australasia (including Australia and New Zealand) with the first white citizens. They were mainly Protestants.
- By 1927 more than 10,000 Greeks had moved to Australia in order to find work. Greek Orthodox churches developed in various cities. Today the Greek Church in Australia has over 100 priests and 105 churches.

Gladys Aylward

Gladys Aylward (1903–70) had been a housemaid. After she became a Christian at the age of 26, she decided she must go to China to tell people about Jesus. Without anybody's help, she travelled across Europe and Asia by train. There she worked for another missionary in the town of Yangcheng. She learned Chinese and journeyed around the villages, telling Bible stories.

When Japan invaded China in 1931, her life and work were under threat but she carried on caring for children who had been made homeless by the war. On one famous occasion, she rescued 100 children and led them to safety through unknown mountainous country. On this journey she became very ill. What's more, the journey took over five weeks. Even so, they reached safety in a place called Sian. There Gladys Aylward started a Christian church for refugees.

Look it Up

23 Missions to the World
24 The Church in Russia
28 The Pentecostal Movement
52 Christianity and Other Faiths

28 The Pentecostal Movement

The Pentecostal Church of God in Christ in Los Angeles has 13,000 members and 155 paid staff members. It costs $8 million a year to run.

Look it Up

Fifty days after the first Easter, the original disciples were in Jerusalem when they felt the Holy Spirit came to them. They then went out into the streets to preach about Jesus – and many foreigners in the city understood them as if they were speaking in their languages or 'tongues'. This event is remembered each year as the Christian festival of Pentecost.

The twentieth century 'Pentecostal' movement began not on that Sunday but on 4 April 1906. The congregation in a church in Los Angeles in the United States of America felt that the Holy Spirit had come upon them, as it had come upon the disciples in Jerusalem at Pentecost. For these Americans, it felt like a new beginning. Because Christians are baptized with water when they join the Church, those American Christians named this new beginning 'baptism in the spirit'.

This new Pentecostal movement spread quickly. Pentecostal churches were started not only in the United States but also in England and Wales, in Scandinavia, Germany, South America and South Africa. However, it was in the United States that they became most popular, especially with black and poor white Americans (who felt they did not 'fit in' in ordinary churches) and with others who did not like the seriousness and set patterns of traditional church services.

Pentecostal church services are often very informal. They include gospel music, spontaneous prayers and powerful sermons. Members of the congregation may talk about their own faith. Frequently, people will start hand-clapping and waving or give shouts of 'hallelujah' when they agree with something that is being said. 'Speaking in tongues' is also regularly a part of Pentecostal services.

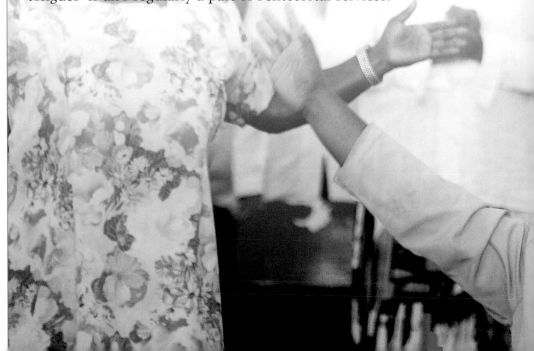

The leader of the church (often called the pastor) may conduct healing ceremonies. Many Pentecostalists believe that illness is the result of sin or wrongdoing. They also believe in prophecy or being able to tell what will happen in the future. Pentecostalists are often fundamentalists; and they are usually against the use of alcohol and tobacco, against dancing and theatre. Most important to them, however, is 'baptism of the spirit' by which they mean a person comes to realise the importance and reality of God.

The growth of the Pentecostal Churches (especially since 1960) has been rapid. Worldwide, there are now more than 200 million committed Pentecostalists. It has come to be seen as a major 'branch' of the Christian Church, alongside the Orthodox, Roman Catholic and Protestant Churches.

There are various groupings within the Pentecostal Churches. In the USA, the primarily black Church of God in Christ has a total of 6.75 million members. Another large grouping is known as the Assemblies of God. There are also the Holiness churches which continue many of John Wesley's Methodist teachings. One of these is the Church of the Nazarene. This Church places great importance on teaching and missionary work, in tithing (giving one tenth of earnings to the Church) and in keeping away from all worldly things. 'Oneness Pentecostals' or 'Jesus-Name Pentecostals' do not believe in the Trinity but believe 'Father', 'Son' and 'Spirit' are titles for God – and that Jesus is another name for God.

Young members of Pentecostal churches parade through Spanish Harlem in New York, USA.

Speaking in Tongues

For Pentecostalists, the gift of 'speaking in tongues' is a sign the Holy Spirit is present and a way of showing they have a close relationship with God. St Paul's letters or epistles show that he had this 'gift of the spirit' and that the groups of Christians to whom he wrote also 'spoke in tongues'.

Sometimes the sounds can be identified as a foreign language. Often it is a collection of spontaneous sounds that cannot be linked to any known language. Some Pentecostalists feel they have the gift of 'interpreting' these sounds or explaining what they mean.

A congregation in a Pentecostal church in Suva on the island of Fiji.

Men and women whose job or life it is to lead or organise a church (or a group of churches) are called the clergy.

29 The Clergy of the Church

Jesus told his disciples that they were to be the servants of others: that they should 'minister' to their needs. These disciples (later called apostles) became the first leaders of the Church. As the Church grew, they chose or elected other leaders and helpers. Some were called deacons. Their work was to help the poor and needy.

Nowadays, after training, a man or woman who is to become one of the clergy is 'ordained' (or 'dedicated' to do God's work) in a special service. The clergy do many different jobs. They lead Sunday and weekday services in churches and chapels. They conduct weddings and funerals. They help people in trouble or need. Some work as teachers in schools. Others work full-or part-time in hospitals, prisons and the armed services. Many clergy are paid for their work but some work voluntarily.

Some clergy wear a special collar so that they can be easily recognized. When they are leading church services, they often wear special clothes called vestments.

Members of the clergy are often given the title 'the Reverend' but across the various Churches, their jobs and ranks have many other different titles.

A woman priest baptizes a newborn baby.

An AIDS patient is given Holy Communion by a Christian minister in Kampala, Uganda.

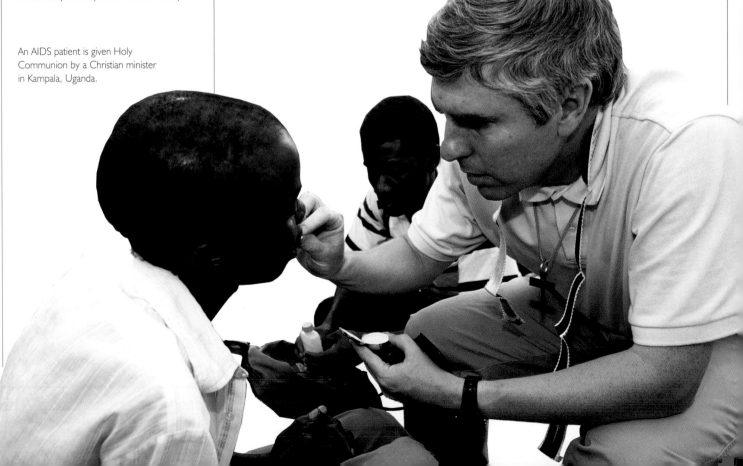

Catholic, Orthodox and Anglican Leaders

In these churches, there are three 'orders' or ranks of clergy. The first has the ancient title of deacon. After one year, most deacons are ordained priests (the second 'order') at a service when a bishop lays his hands on their heads as a sign they are being set apart for their special work. Bishops form the third order. They are senior priests, in charge of all the churches in one area. An archbishop is a senior bishop, in charge of the Church for a large part or the whole of a country. Priests and bishops in Catholic churches are often called 'Father' by their congregations.

Above, bishops of the Church of England wear 'western' type mitres.

Catholic priests are not allowed to marry so that they do not become distracted by family life.

In the Orthodox Church, senior archbishops are called patriarchs; in the Roman Catholic Church, they are called cardinals. Cardinals elect the pope, the head of the Roman Catholic Church. In the Anglican Church, a priest who runs one church (or more) is called a vicar or rector. A priest who works in a school, hospital, prison or the armed services is called chaplain.

A Greek Orthodox bishop, wearing red and gold festive vestments and mitre like a crown.

Protestant Churches

The Protestant Churches do not use the word 'priest', preferring a title such as minister or pastor. The word pastor originally meant a shepherd, someone who cares for his flock.

Lay Workers

Christians who are not ordained are called 'lay' members of the Church. Many commit a lot of time and effort to helping people in their faith and to community projects.

These Scottish children learn about the faith at Sunday school. Their teacher is probably a lay worker – not one of the clergy.

Look it Up

5 The Ministry of Jesus;
17 The Roman Catholic Church;
35 Inside an Orthodox Church;
55 The Divided Church

Over the years, Christians have erected special buildings in which to meet and worship – buildings usually called churches.

Many builders meant their churches to teach a lesson. This city centre church has a short spire – but it is still meant to lift the eyes of the passer-by up towards heaven.

30 Church Buildings

Churches vary enormously. Some are huge, some tiny. Some are dark and mysterious, others bright and airy. They may be beautifully decorated with stained glass windows, statues and other ornaments – or very plain and simple. Some of the churches we see today are hundreds of years old while others have been built in modern times. Christians have often spent a great deal of money on their church buildings. They say that only the best is good enough for God's home on earth. Others believe that elaborate decoration is a waste of money, distracting or unnecessary.

Whatever churches look like, their purpose is the same. They are places where Christians can meet together to worship God and share their love and friendship with one another.

Many churches have been built in the shape of a cross, as a reminder of how Jesus died. The head or 'top' of the cross usually points east towards the rising sun. Some people say this is because Jesus is a light coming into the world; others say it is because European Christians wanted their churches to point east towards Jerusalem.

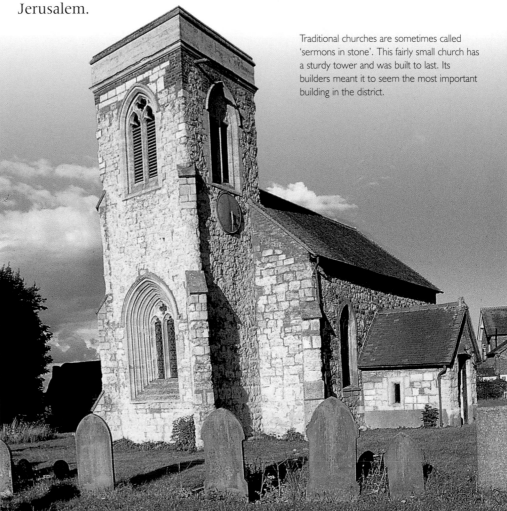

Traditional churches are sometimes called 'sermons in stone'. This fairly small church has a sturdy tower and was built to last. Its builders meant it to seem the most important building in the district.

Look it Up

Many churches have tall, pointed spires or square towers. In either case, the idea of this is to lift everyone's eyes up to heaven – which people used to believe was a place above the sky. Usually, bells were hung in church towers. In the days when people had no watches, the bells rang out when it was time to go to church.

For Roman Catholics and Anglicans the main church of an area (or diocese) is called its cathedral – like Canterbury Cathedral, shown in chapter 21. In it will be a special chair or throne used by the bishop of that diocese. The Latin name for this seat is *cathedra* – a word which gives us the name for this 'mother' church of an area.

Protestants sometimes use the word chapel to describe their meeting place. A chapel can also mean a small church or a church which is part of a school, hospital or prison.

This English church has a timber frame and thatched roof – a traditional building style for homes and farms in the area, and which makes the building look like it belongs to the community.

Although this church in France is of a very modern design, its dignified shape still lifts the eyes upwards.

Ever since Christianity became legal within the Roman empire, its followers have met together inside special buildings to worship God.

Vestments

In many Catholic and Anglican churches, the special vestments worn by the priest during services and the covers on the front of the altar will be changed to show the different seasons of the year. During Christmas and Easter, they will be white or gold. During the serious seasons of Advent and Lent they are violet (purple). At Pentecost and on some other special days they are red. During the rest of the year (sometimes called 'Ordinary Time'), they are green.

Look it Up

31  Inside a Church

In Roman Catholic and Anglican (or Episcopalian) church buildings, the main feature is the altar or holy table, used in Holy Communion services. It used to be always placed at the eastern end of the building in the 'top' arm of the cross. This part of the church is called the chancel. In it, there may be benches ('stalls') where the choir sits – and also an organ. Nowadays, the altar may be in the middle of the church.

In the main body of the church (the nave) are benches (known as pews) or ordinary chairs for the people to sit on. Facing them, there is usually a stand (called a lectern) from where the Bible is read aloud. Sometimes this is in the shape of an eagle, the idea being that this great bird is carrying the word of God into the world. There will also be a raised stand or pulpit in which the priest can stand to preach or teach the people. Any passageway down the centre of the church is known as an aisle.

There may be one or more side rooms called vestries where the clergy and choir may gather and get ready before a service begins.

At the west end of the church is a font where baptisms may take place.

In medieval times, churches were meeting places and many different events took place inside them. This is now happening again. More and more churches are used during the week for meetings and for teaching. Some churches open to offer refreshments to their members and to those in need.

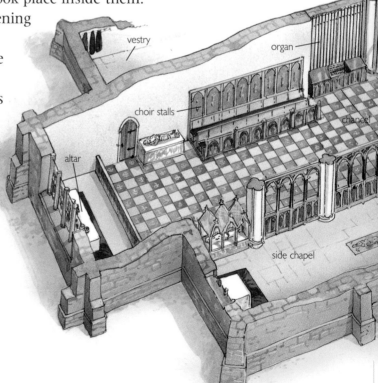

This circular church was specially designed to make the pulpit the most important and visible part of the building.

Preaching the Word

In Protestant churches (where preaching and Bible reading is especially important), the pulpit is often in the centre of the building.

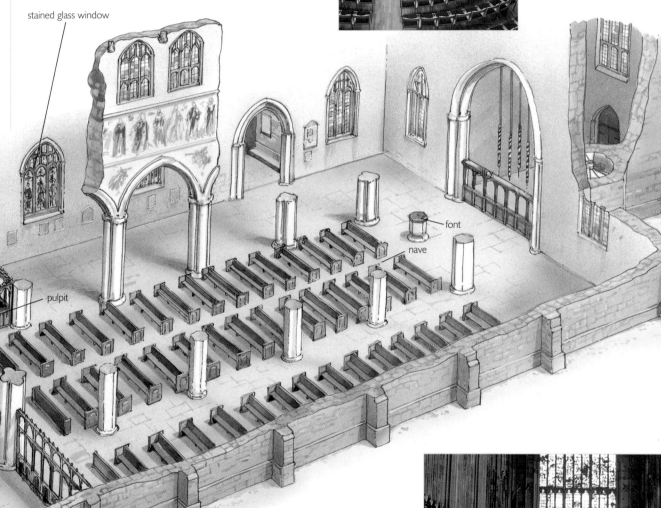

stained glass window

belfry

font

nave

pulpit

The lectern is usually the opposite side of the church to the pulpit. However, it can be found in other places. This lectern, in King's College Chapel, Cambridge, England, is in the centre of the nave.

Over the centuries, Christians have used different forms of art to make clear the stories of their faith and its teachings.

32 Christian Art

The Jewish religion teaches that it is wrong to make any images: there should be no pictures or statues of holy objects or of God or indeed of any living thing. Because the first Christians were Jews, they followed this rule – which is why we have no picture or painting of Jesus made in his own lifetime.

Over the next few centuries, Christians began to change their minds and to create religious paintings, mosaics and statues of Jesus and the apostles. Many came to believe that, as churches and cathedrals were God's 'houses on earth', they should look as splendid as possible – so they made pictures and carvings showing not only Jesus and his followers but other stories from the Bible and other respected Christians such as the saints.

The Cross

In most churches there is at least one cross, the Christian symbol, which is a reminder to Christians of how Jesus suffered for their sake. Some Christians bow or nod to the cross – not because they worship that image of a cross but as a sign that they are remembering how Jesus died on a cross.

Crosses are not all the same. Some are plain, bare crosses; others (called crucifixes) show Jesus suffering on the cross. Some show Jesus as a king who has triumphed over the suffering of the world.

Look it Up

Stained Glass

In the days when ordinary people could not read, stained glass windows in churches helped them learn the teachings of their religion and the stories of the Bible – in the same way that the size of large churches taught them the importance of God. This stained glass window shows the miraculous catch of fish by the disciples. (Luke 5:1–11.)

At the time of the Reformation, many Protestant reformers felt statues, stained glass windows and paintings distracted people from the worship of God. They also felt that such pictures and carvings were 'graven images' which people might worship. (The second of the ten commandments in the Bible teaches that it is wrong to worship any image.) As a result, many windows and carvings were destroyed. From then on, Protestant places of worship (like this chapel in Hawaii) were often much plainer and simpler with fewer decorations.

Art for the World

In the last 100 years, different artists around the world have found their own ways of illustrating Bible stories, often showing these stories as if they were happening in their local setting. This twentieth-century crucifix from Nigeria shows Jesus as an African.

Frescoes

Artists have painted many scenes from Bible stories – sometimes directly onto the walls and ceilings of churches, as the Italian painter Michelangelo did in the Sistine Chapel in Rome. These are called frescoes.

The ceiling of the Sistine Chapel (above) was painted between 1508 and 1512. The nine central frescoes show scenes from Genesis, including scenes from the story of God's creation of the world, and the stories of Adam and Eve, and Noah and the flood.

For Christians, prayer means talking to God – and also listening to him.

Saying Grace

Some families say a prayer together, before a meal, to thank God for their food and drink. This is sometimes called 'saying grace'. They may use words like either of these two 'graces':

*'For food and friends,
Lord, we thank you.'*

*'For what we are about to receive,
may the Lord make us truly
thankful.'*

Look it Up

33 Private and Public Prayer

Several times in the Gospels we are told that Jesus went away from his followers to pray privately and quietly on his own. Christians also do this. They may pray each morning or evening, perhaps at their bedside. Christians believe that it is possible to pray anywhere and at any time and that God will hear them.

For the Christian, prayer is not just a matter of asking God for things. It can include:
- Praising God for his greatness (Praise)
- Thanking God for gifts such as food and health (Thanksgiving)
- Saying sorry for having done wrong things (Confession)
- Asking for God's help for other people, especially loved ones and the sick (Intercession)
- Asking for help for oneself (Petition).

For their private prayers, some Christians use books of printed prayers but many simply talk to God in their own words. Many Christians also say a short private prayer at particular moments during the day when they want God's help. These little prayers are sometimes called 'arrow prayers' because the person saying them hopes their words will 'fly' to God like an arrow.

For Christians, prayer also means listening to God. Many believe that God 'talks' to them, not in a voice out loud that they can actually hear, but by giving them a strong feeling that they should do something in particular.

This Indian woman is praying with a rosary: she says a set prayer as she holds each bead in turn and at the same time reflects on the life of Jesus.

The Lord's Prayer

During his 'Sermon on the Mount', Jesus told his followers how they should pray. He told them not to use a lot of meaningless words but to say this prayer to God the Father. The prayer he gave them is recorded in Matthew's Gospel and also in Luke. It has become known as the Lord's Prayer or the 'Our Father' (because of its first two words) and Christians may say it privately or together in public church services. Here is a version from a present-day prayerbook.

Our Father in heaven,
hallowed be your name,
your kingdom come,
your will be done,
on earth as [it is] in heaven.
Give us today our daily bread.
Forgive us our sins
as we forgive those who sin against us.
Lead us not into temptation
but deliver us from evil.

This ancient ending is often said:

For the kingdom, the power,
and the glory are yours
now and for ever. Amen.

The word 'Amen' is a Hebrew word meaning 'So be it' and ends most Christian prayers.

Catholic Christians (and others) may go to church to make a private confession to the priest. They often do this on a Saturday evening as a way of preparing for the main service on Sunday.

Public Prayer

On one occasion, Jesus told his followers this: 'Whenever two of you… agree about anything you pray for, it will be done for you by my Father in heaven. For where two or three come together in my name, I am there with them.' (Matthew 18:19.)

Christians have always met to say prayers together. Usually this happens in church services but groups may also gather together in one of their homes for a 'prayer meeting' when they can share their concerns or worries.

Jesus told his closest followers that they had the authority to forgive sins. Many Christians believe that this power has been passed on to today's bishops and priests. For this reason, in many churches, the bishop or priest will 'pronounce absolution'. This means that, after the people have confessed their sins to God, the priest says a prayer giving them God's forgiveness.

This happens during church services, especially Holy Communion services.

The Jesus Prayer

One prayer (which originated in Orthodox Churches) has been in use for centuries. It is called the Jesus Prayer:

'Lord Jesus Christ,
Son of God, be merciful to me,
a sinner.'

At his last supper with his closest followers, Jesus told them to 'do this' in his memory.

34 Holy Communion

The night before Jesus was crucified, he had a last supper with his closest friends, or 'disciples'. At that meal, he took the bread, gave thanks to God, broke the bread and shared it with his disciples. 'Take, eat,' he said. 'This is my body which is given for you.'

Then he took a cup of wine, again gave thanks, and gave it to each of them to drink. 'This is my blood,' he said, 'which is shed for you and for many.' Jesus then told his followers to 'do this in remembrance of me'.

This story is told in the Gospels of Matthew, Mark and Luke and we know that the very first Christians carried out Jesus' command. The apostle Paul mentions it in his letters (or epistles), showing that the early Christian Churches followed this instruction. Ever since, Christians have met to do this in church services often called Holy Communion.

Going to Holy Communion is a very important act for a Christian. Many go every Sunday. Some go on other special days as well, such as their birthday or saints' days and other holy days. A few go every day. Others go more rarely: perhaps only two or three times a year, because they believe that such a service is so special it should not be allowed to become 'ordinary'.

Names for the Service

Different Churches use different names for the service of Holy Communion.

Eucharist: *Eucharist* is a Greek word meaning 'thanksgiving'. This name shows that the service is a thanksgiving for the life and sacrifice of Jesus. If there is music and singing at the service as well, it may be called 'Sung Eucharist'.

Holy Communion: This name shows that, in this service, Christians meet together, with Jesus, as a community at the altar.

Lord's Supper: This name emphasizes the memory of the last supper.

Mass: This name is used especially in the Roman Catholic Church. It comes from the last sentence of the Latin version of the Catholic form of service: *ite missa est* ('you are dismissed').

At the Service

In some churches (especially in Greek Orthodox ones but increasingly in others as well), the bread and wine are brought by people attending the service as an act of thanksgiving. In other churches (such as the Roman Catholic Church and in some Anglican churches), special wafers are used instead of ordinary bread.

The Holy Communion usually begins with the people confessing their sins. There will then be Bible readings and prayers. There may also be hymns and other music.

At the most holy moment of the service the priest or minister stands at the altar and says a prayer over the bread and wine, recalling what happened at the Last Supper and the words Jesus said.

Then the people come to kneel or stand at the altar to receive the elements – a piece of bread and a sip of wine.

A young girl makes her first communion in Malaga, Spain.

The Meaning of the Service

For some Christians, the service is a memorial, a reminder of the sacrifice made by Jesus on the cross.

For Roman Catholics, Orthodox Christians and others, it is much more. They believe that when the priest says the prayer over the body and wine, they become (in some mysterious way) the body and blood of Jesus – so that in receiving Holy Communion, they are receiving Jesus into their soul.

Sacraments

The service of Holy Communion is also known as a 'sacrament'. A sacrament is an act with an outward sign which has an 'inner', special meaning (remembering or receiving Christ).

For most Christians, there is another sacrament, Baptism, at which water is the outward sign of the inner meaning: that God is now present with the person being baptized. Most Christians believe that these two sacraments (Baptism and Holy Communion) are a necessary part of being a good Christian.

Roman Catholic and Orthodox Christians say there are five other sacraments but these are not necessary for all Christians: Confirmation; Confession; Holy Unction; Ordination; and Marriage.

Look it Up

**41 Infant Baptism
and Rites of Passage
(Confirmation)
33 Private and Public Prayer
(Confession)
46 Death: in Sure and Certain Hope
(Holy Unction)
29 The Clergy of the Church
(Ordination)
42: Marriage**

**See also:
6 The Death and Resurrection
of Jesus
31 Inside a Church**

This fresco or wall painting showing the Eucharist or Holy Communion dates from the third century and shows how important the service has always been to many Christians.

Heavenly Words

Buildings and the clergy of the Orthodox Church are richly decorated to help the congregation think about the majesty and splendor of God. Many Orthodox prayers paint similar pictures with the words they use. Here is one:

Glory to the Father, who has woven
  garments of glory for the
  resurrection;
worship to the Son, who was
  clothed in them at his rising;
thanksgiving to the Sprit, who
  keeps them all for the saints;
one nature in three, to him
  be praise.

Syrian Orthodox Church

The priest chants the words of the service and the people answer in song.

35 Inside an Orthodox Church

Orthodox churches are usually built in the shape of a square cross (like a plus sign) with a dome in the centre of the roof. The cross shape reminds people of the crucifixion. The dome reminds them of heaven and may be decorated with holy pictures.

Every Sunday and on other holy days, Orthodox Christians hold their most important service, the Divine Liturgy. It can last several hours and in it are remembered (in turn) the birth, life, death and resurrection of Jesus. It includes prayers, chanting, readings from the Bible and Holy Communion. The word 'liturgy' (used of a public act of worship) means 'order of service'.

Musical instruments are rarely used in Orthodox churches.

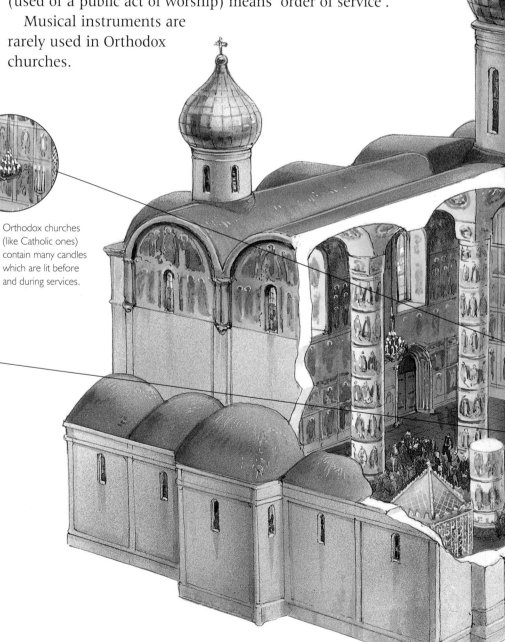

Orthodox churches (like Catholic ones) contain many candles which are lit before and during services.

In the screen are doors leading into the sanctuary. They are normally kept shut as a reminder that people are cut off from God by their sins. Only the priests may go through them. The opening of the doors teaches that God has opened a door that allows people to be joined with God through the sacrifice of Jesus on the cross.

• There are usually few chairs in an Orthodox church. The people stand and move around the church during the service, bowing and kissing the icons as a mark of respect and saying their prayers before them. During a service they may move across the church to greet friends they suddenly notice or to light a candle and place it on one of the stands.

The altar stands in the most holy part of the church, called the sanctuary. It is hidden from the people by a screen. This screen is called the iconostasis because it is covered with holy pictures called icons. These are often surrounded with gold paint.

The Divine Liturgy

During the Divine Liturgy, the priest carries bread and wine through the screen into the sanctuary. He places them on the altar and prayers are said. When he brings them back into the nave, Orthodox Christians believe the bread and wine have become the body and blood of Jesus. After a silence, hymns are sung and bells are rung in joyful celebration.

• Those receiving Holy Communion normally will have eaten nothing since the night before. They receive a portion of the holy bread which has been dipped in the wine and placed in a spoon. Other Christians and visitors may be invited to receive a piece of bread which has been blessed (but not placed on the altar) as a sign of fellowship.

The main part of the church, or nave, is square shaped.

Look it Up

Since the earliest days of Christianity, music has been a part of public worship.

36 Church Music

In the Gospels we read that Jesus and his disciples sang a hymn at the Last Supper. It may well have been one of the psalms or songs which form part of the Old Testament and which are part of Jewish worship.

Around the year 600 CE, Pope Gregory I created the first school to train groups or choirs of singers to lead the singing during church services. Over the years, many churches and cathedrals have trained their own choirs – as they still do today.

Pope Gregory also encouraged the use of chants now known as plainsong or Gregorian chant. Many monasteries became famous for their singing. Plainsong does not need musical instruments as an accompaniment.

Gospel Music

In the twentieth century, Pentecostal and other Protestant churches began using lively music, sometimes accompanied by bands and large choirs, in their services. Churches (especially in the United States) with mainly black congregations created new 'Gospel music' which praises God while teaching the Gospel message and asking for social justice.

A group of monks sing a hymn and wave palm branches as they walk through Jerusalem on Palm Sunday.

The Psalms

One of the books in the Old Testament is the Book of Psalms. It contains 150 songs of praise and prayer and a few of them may have been written by King David, one of the leaders of the Jewish people. The word 'psalm' is of later origin: it comes from a Greek word meaning a song accompanied by a harp.

Christians continue to chant psalms in many of their services today and many Christians say favourite ones as part of their private prayers. A particular favourite is Psalm 23, which is a song of praise for the way God cares for his people. It begins:

> The Lord is my shepherd, I shall not want.
> He makes me lie down in green pastures;
> he leads me beside still waters;
> he restores my soul.

After the Reformation, many psalms were rewritten so that they rhymed and would fit tunes that were easier to sing. This happened especially in Swiss Protestant Churches and also in the Scottish Presbyterian Church. This is the beginning of the same psalm from the 1650 'Scottish Psalter':

> The Lord's my Shepherd, I'll not want.
> He makes me down to lie
> In pastures green; he leadeth me
> The quiet waters by.

This manuscript shows how early church music was written down and illustrated by monks.

However, organs soon became a feature of churches and were played to help guide the singing.

With the Reformation, the new Protestant groups not only wanted their churches to be plainer and free of statues and other decorations, they also wanted to rid them of organs – and many church organs were destroyed. Even so, the early Protestants continued to sing or chant hymns and psalms as part of their services.

Meanwhile, for the Roman Catholic Church during the 1600s and 1700s, famous composers such as Bach and Mozart wrote great musical works (including musical settings of the mass) which were sung by cathedral and other large choirs accompanied by organs or even whole orchestras.

Gradually, the Protestant Churches began to reintroduce church music and many new hymns were written for ordinary Christians to sing in both Catholic and Protestant churches.

Charles Wesley

One famous hymn writer was the brother of the preacher John Wesley. Charles Wesley had to stop travelling with John in 1756 because of poor health. He then began writing hymns and, during the rest of his life, he wrote over 6,000. One of his best known is the Christmas carol, 'Hark, the Herald Angels sing'. Another is a hymn about God's love: 'Love divine, all loves excelling…'

Look it Up

Christians remember events in the life of Jesus at particular times of the year.

Christian Festivals

As the Christian religion spread through the Roman empire, its teachers tried to persuade people to give up their old pagan celebrations. To help them do this, different Christian festivals were celebrated at the time of year particular pagan festivals had taken place. So, for example, Christians began celebrating Christmas at the time of an earlier, pagan mid-winter festival.

The festivals from Advent to Ascension Day mark the events of the life of Jesus. Then, at Pentecost, Christians think about the coming of the Holy Spirit.

Catholics and some other Christians also observe certain festivals that recall events in the life of Mary, the mother of Jesus.

On All Saints' Day, Christians (especially Catholic Christians) give thanks for all the good people who have lived in the past. The next day is called All Souls' Day, on which prayers are offered for friends and relatives who have died.

Look it Up

37 The Christian Year

For many Christians, their main festival happens every Sunday when they remember and celebrate the resurrection of Jesus Christ. This was certainly the case for the first Christians but, as the years passed, the Church began to make a special, annual observance of that event called Easter. In the year 325 CE, a way of working out when Easter should be celebrated was decided upon.

Christmas and other festivals and fasts came into being later.

● Advent

Advent comes from a Latin word meaning 'coming' or arrival and so Advent is often said to be a time of waiting or preparation for the coming of Jesus to earth as a baby at Christmas.

In some churches and homes, there will be an Advent wreath with five candles: one coloured one for each of the four Sundays in Advent and one white one which stands for Jesus, who is said to be 'the light of the world'. This white candle is not lit until Christmas Day.

○ Christmas

For Christians, this festival only really begins on Christmas Eve – and then lasts for the following twelve days.

For all Christians in the southern half of the world, Christmas is a summer, not a winter, festival.

◐ Orthodox Christmas

The Russian, Armenian and some other Orthodox Churches use a much older calendar (known as the Julian Calendar) than the one used in western countries (known as the Gregorian Calendar). There are now thirteen days difference between the two calendars so for those Churches using the Julian calendar, '25 December' (and therefore Christmas Day) happens on what the western world knows as 7 January.

◑ Epiphany

After the twelve days of Christmas comes Epiphany, which celebrates the visit of wise men to the baby Jesus. Epiphany comes from a Greek word meaning 'showing'. This was the first 'showing' of Jesus to non-Jewish people.

Lent

For Christians, Lent is a time of fasting and preparation for Easter. It begins with Ash Wednesday, a day when some churches hold a service during which a smudge of ash is put on people's foreheads as a sign they are sorry for the wrong things they have done.

Holy Week

The week immediately before Easter is called Holy Week. It begins with Palm Sunday and includes Maundy Thursday (which marks Jesus' Last Supper) and Good Friday, when Christians remember the crucifixion.

Easter

Easter Day is followed by 40 days of rejoicing. During this period, a large candle known as a Pascal Candle is lit in some churches. Pascal is another word for Easter.

Ascension Day

Ascension Day marks the last time the disciples of Jesus saw the man some call 'the king of the world'.

Pentecost (or Whitsun)

Ten days after Ascension comes Pentecost which marks the coming of the Holy Spirit to the eleven faithful disciples.

Young children act out the Christmas story in a school in Honolulu, Hawaii.

A Palm Sunday procession in San Salvador, El Salvador, in which a statue of Jesus is carried through the streets.

Liturgical Seasons and Colours

There is a pattern to the use of liturgical colours.

         (○)

| **Advent** and **Lent** are seasons of fasting and penitence. The chuch and clergy may wear violet. | **Christmas**, **Easter** and **Trinity Sunday** are times of celebration. The colours worn are white or gold. | **Pentecost** and some special days such as saint's days are celebrated with red. | Other times – **Ordinary Time** – are decked in green – the colour of growth. These are times for teaching and learning – growing in the faith. |

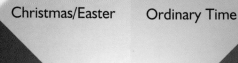

Christmas/Easter   Ordinary Time

Advent/Lent   Special Days

This Easter procession happens on the island of Sicily, Italy.

79

The saints are those who hold a special position in Christian history and in people's hearts.

38  Saints of the Christian Church

For some Christians, a saint is anyone who truly believes that Jesus is the Son of God and who tries to follow his teaching. In his letters or epistles, St Paul writes about the 'saints' at Ephesus, Philippi and Colossae. By this, he means all the Christians in those cities.

For other Christians a 'saint' is a very good or holy person who has died and is believed to be in heaven. That person is thought special because God gave him or her a special gift. It might be the gift of loving God; the gift of healing or teaching; the gift of bravery or patience; the gift of wisdom; or the gift of being able to love the friendless or needy. Christians call this gift 'grace'. The word 'saint' comes from the Latin *sanctus*, which means 'holy'.

Who are Saints?

Catholic and Orthodox Christians give the title 'saint' to a person after they have died if their Church decides that person deserves the title. In the Orthodox Church, a person is named a saint by a group of local bishops.

In the Roman Catholic Church, people are remembered as saints if they have been 'canonized'. Church leaders investigate if the person really had done something miraculous or out of the ordinary. If the answer is yes, the pope canonizes the person and they are then known as 'Saint …'.

Both Catherine of Alexandria (left) and Lawrence of Rome were made saints because they were put to death for their faith.

Look it Up

4 The First Christmas
37 The Christian Year

Many Christians – especially Catholic Christians – believe that the saints watch over, pray for and protect those living on earth. Each person is in the special care of their patron saint (the saint on whose day they were born or whom they were named after). Some Christians celebrate their saint's day (or 'name day') rather like an extra birthday.

It is also said that particular saints offer special help according to our homeland or circumstances. For example, the patron saint of bus drivers is St Christopher and the patron saint of scientists is St Albert the Great, a German who wrote many books on physics and who gave up being a bishop because he thought he would be 'more useful teaching in schools'.

Some Christians pray to the saints, asking for their help because they believe the saints are close to God. Just as they might ask a friend to pray for them, so they ask a saint in heaven for the same blessing.

Each saint is remembered on a particular day of the year.

St Christopher is popularly believed to be the patron saint of travellers.

A carving in a south London church of Jesus on the cross, watched by Mary his mother.

Mary the Mother of Jesus

Because Mary was chosen by God to be the mother of Jesus, most Christians respect Mary. But many of these Christians say that, although she was special, it is not necessary to pray to her. All prayers should be said directly to God, 'through Jesus Christ'.

Roman Catholic Christians (and some others) believe that, because Mary was so close to Jesus, it is right to ask 'Our Lady' to pray to Jesus on their behalf.

One prayer they say is known as the 'Hail Mary':

Hail Mary, full of grace, blessed are you among women
And blessed is the fruit of your womb, Jesus.
Holy Mary, Mother of God,
Pray for us sinners now and at the hour of our death.

Some Christians believe that Mary had no other children but Jesus. They talk of her as the 'Blessed Virgin Mary'. Others point out that three of the Gospels (Matthew, Mark and Luke) all mention a time Jesus was teaching and 'his mother and brothers' came to see him (Matthew 12:46, Mark 3:21, Luke 8:19) This suggests Mary had other children after Jesus.

Mary is remembered especially on 25 March each year, a day sometimes known as the Annunciation. Nine months before Christmas Day, it is celebrated as the day the angel Gabriel announced to Mary she would be the mother of Jesus. The first line of the 'Hail Mary' is the first line of Gabriel's announcement from Luke's Gospel.

Many church services once followed quite strict patterns. Nowadays they vary much more.

House Churches

For many years, Christians have met together in small groups to pray and study the Bible. Sometimes these groups contain members of different denominations or churches but, in the last 50 years, some of these groups have become actual 'house churches', using a group member's home for worship rather than going to a special church building.

Besides praying together, the house church group may tell each other the things they want to thank God for or they may share their problems. In some cases, they may remember Jesus' Last Supper by sharing bread and wine.

Charismatic pilgrims carry a statue of Mary in a procession in Chile, South America.

Look it Up

39 New Ways to Worship

In modern times, Christians have felt free to worship God in new ways. One way has become known as the charismatic movement. The word 'charismatic' comes from a Greek word meaning 'favour' or 'grace'.

In some ways, the charismatic movement is closely linked to the Pentecostal Churches. 'Charismatic' church services (like Pentecostal ones) often include speaking in tongues, lively music, enthusiastic impromptu or unplanned talks and prayers, the practice of healing and other 'gifts of the Spirit'. But since the early 1960s, many members of the more traditional Churches have experienced these 'gifts of the Spirit' and charismatic services can now be found in Lutheran, Baptist, Anglican, Mennonite and even Roman Catholic churches.

Charismatic Christians are usually strict in the way they behave and are keen to share the 'good news' or Gospel with non-believers and give themselves wholeheartedly to their faith.

The charismatic movement has flourished in Central and Southern America, in Africa and Asia and in the countries that once made up the Soviet Union. It now has at least 500 million followers.

Some churches and cathedrals hold special services for young people using types of modern popular music that will appeal to them. This one is in Ely Cathedral, England.

Some churches run special courses to help people to find out about the faith and to encourage them to attend church regularly and to feel part of the 'church family'. For example, the Cursillo Movement (which began in the 1940s in Spain) is now a worldwide movement which aims to help its followers to be better Catholics by being more like Jesus in their daily lives. The word *cursillo* means 'short course': many followers of the movement begin by joining a short course to learn more about its aims. A Protestant movement which began in England but is now becoming a worldwide one is known as the Alpha Course. Such courses may be for those who know very little about Christianity or church members who want to know more.

Other churches hold special services for young people using types of modern popular music that will appeal to them.

Televangelists

Since the 1960s, the spread of television and especially cable television has brought many more channels into being. Some Christians (especially in the United States of America) have chosen to use them to set up television stations on which to spread the teachings of Jesus.

Most of these Christian networks are Protestant and evangelical (that is, they place emphasis on spreading the word of God). One preacher frequently puts it in these words: 'We have a biblical duty, we are called by God, to conquer this country.' The preachers have become known as 'televangelists' and many are fundamentalists. One of the biggest stations is the Trinity Broadcasting Network, which originated in the United States but now also broadcasts across Europe and the Middle East in various languages and also in Australia. Viewers are invited to phone in their prayers or to convert to Christianity.

There are also a number of Roman Catholic channels.

Most of the televangelists appeal on screen for money to run their television stations and some have built large churches which serve the Christians who worship in them and, at the same time, are television studios.

The ceremony or service during which a person becomes a member of the Christian church is called baptism.

Baptism

The word 'baptism' originally meant 'washing' or 'immersion'.

Another word for baptism is 'christening', though this usually refers just to infant baptism.

Baptism by 'immersion' (above) in a First African Baptist church in Savannah, Georgia, USA; and (right) at an open-air baptism service outside an Anglican church in York, England, led by the Archbishop of York.

40 Believers' Baptism

Jesus' final instructions to his disciples, according to the Gospel of St Matthew, were these:

'Go then, to all people everywhere and make them my disciples: baptize them in the name of the Father, the Son and the Holy Spirit, and teach them to obey everything I have commanded you.'
Matthew 28:19–20.

The book of Acts describes their first successes. After Peter preached on the day of Pentecost, 3,000 asked to be baptized as believers. When Philip was on the road from Jerusalem to Gaza he met an Ethiopian official and so convinced him about Jesus that the man asked for his carriage to be stopped so he could be baptized in a pool of water by the side of the road. Believers' baptism has been a central part of Christian practice from the beginning and through the early centuries of the faith.

However, the book of Acts also tells of how Peter was invited to the home of a Roman official named Cornelius. When Cornelius believed, he asked not only for himself but for all his household to be baptized. This set an example for baptizing babies: the grown-ups in a household promised to raise the child in the faith and to make baptism the sign of that promise.

To this day, many Churches (such as the Roman Catholic and several Protestant Churches) baptize children while they are babies. However, some of the Reformation Churches, including Baptists and Anabaptists, are among those Christians who think that believers'

John the Baptist

Jesus had a cousin called John. John was six months older than Jesus. When John grew up, he went to live in a desert area some way from Jerusalem and near the River Jordan. He dressed in a tunic made out of camel's hair and lived on honey and flying insects called locusts.

John bathed or baptized people in the Jordan. At that time, baptism was a way that non-Jewish people could become members of the Jewish religion. It showed that a person was making a new start: their previous sin or wrongdoing was being 'washed away'.

Many people went out to see John. Some thought he looked how the prophets must have looked in olden times and wondered if he might be 'the promised one' – 'Messiah' – that God had said would one day save the Jewish people from their troubles and free them from Roman rule. John immediately denied this. He said, 'I baptize you with water, but among you stands the one you do not know. He is coming after me, but I am not good enough even to untie his sandals… He is greater than I am… He is the one who baptizes with the Holy Spirit.' (John 1:26, 30, 33.)

That man was Jesus, who came to be baptized by John in the Jordan at the start of his own ministry – even though (as John said) he had no need to be baptized. It became the sign of his new ministry of preaching.

John baptized Jesus in the River Jordan. To this day, some Christians try to use a river for their services of believers' baptism. Some pilgrims even make the journey to the Holy Land to be baptized in the Jordan itself.

baptism is the right thing to do. They baptize only people who have decided for themselves that they want to be baptized.

The person being baptized is completely immersed in a bath of water for a few seconds (just as Jesus was immersed by John in the River Jordan). This total immersion is a sign all past sins are being washed away.

In some Baptist churches, there is a tiled pool in front of the pulpit with steps leading down into it. After each person has said they believe in Jesus and promised to follow him and serve God, they walk down the steps into the water and are gently lowered under the water for a moment.

In some places, open water such as a river or lake is chosen for a baptism ceremony.

Although Christians do not agree on the time and method of baptism, almost all believe it is an important stage in the Christian life.

Other Denominations

Two Christian denominations do not believe in baptism: the Salvation Army and the Society of Friends.

Look it Up

41 Infant Baptism and Rites of Passage

Parents who believe in infant baptism do so because they believe it is good to be a Christian and want their child to grow up as a member of the Christian Church. In the Roman Catholic and Anglican Churches, it happens in similar ways. Baptism (or Christening) is the time when that baby is given his or her Christian name in the sight of God and becomes a member of the Church.

It usually takes place in church at the font. In many churches, this is a large stone basin standing on a carved pedestal. It is placed near the entrance of a church to show that baptism marks the entry of a person into membership of the church.

A baby is baptized and received into membership of an African church.

First Communion

In the Roman Catholic Church, the next step after baptism on a young Christian's journey through life comes when that child makes his or her first confession and then receives Holy Communion for the first time. This is an important occasion for the whole family and the children making their first communion often wear special new white clothes.

In the Orthodox Church, children receive communion from the time they are old enough to eat.

Children walk in procession through the streets of Positano in Italy to receive their first Communion.

Confirmation

In Roman Catholic and Anglican Churches, there is a service called Confirmation when young people or adults who were baptized as babies take upon themselves the promises and responsibilities of being full members of their Church. This service is usually led by a bishop, who lays his hands on the heads of those being confirmed, blessing them as members of the Church. Sometimes an adult who was not baptized as a baby may be both baptized and confirmed at the same time.

The word 'confirm' means to make strong. Confirmation is a reminder of how, in the very early days of the church, after people were baptized as Christians, one of the apostles 'laid their hands upon them' in blessing.

In the Roman Catholic and Anglican Churches, confirmation usually happens between the ages of 10 and 14 but may happen when a person is an adult. Some Protestant churches (such as the Methodist and Pentecostal Churches) do not have confirmation but have their own services during which new members are received into the church.

In the Orthodox Church, confirmation happens immediately after infant baptism. The priest takes holy oil and uses it to make the sign of the cross on the baby's forehead, eyelids, nostrils, ears, lips, chest, hands and feet.

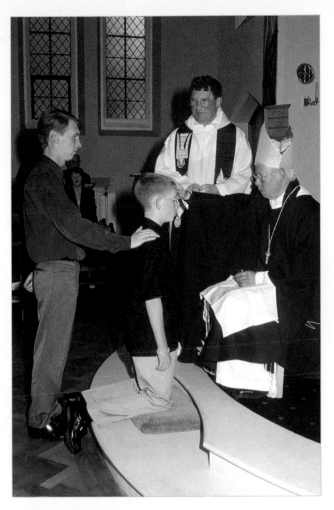

A bishop confirms a young member of a Roman Catholic church in London, England.

At the font, the priest asks if the child will be brought up as a Christian. The priest then makes the sign of the cross on the baby's forehead. A little water is poured over the baby's forehead as the priest says (using the baby's Christian name), '......, I baptize you in the name of the Father, and of the Son, and of the Holy Spirit.' Following this, the newly baptized child is welcomed into the worldwide Christian Church. Orthodox Churches have their own tradition: a baby is baptized by being plunged three times into a bowl of holy water.

In some churches, baptism is a separate service. Nowadays, many churches are returning to an earlier custom of holding baptisms during ordinary Sunday services. In this way, the baby can be welcomed into the church by the wider family of Christian believers.

Look it Up

6 The Death and Resurrection of Jesus
7 The First Christians
21 Differing Denominations
22 North American Protestants
40 Believers' Baptism

42 Marriage

When two Christians decide they want to get married, they almost always feel that they want to make promises about loving and caring for each other in church and with God's blessing. Many other people who do not regularly go to church still feel that a church is the right place in which to make such solemn promises (called 'vows').

In most European countries and in the United States of America, there must be a civil, legal registration of a marriage as well as any church ceremony.

The Church Ceremony

Until the Reformation, the man and the woman exchanged their vows and were married outside the church, at its doorway. They then went inside for a Holy Communion service – also called a 'nuptial' (wedding)

Orthodox Weddings

Different branches of the Christian church celebrate weddings in slightly different ways. In the Orthodox Church, the couple often make a circular procession around the inside of the church to show that marriage (like a circle) has no end. They may also wear crowns to show their importance to each other.

Look it Up

34 Holy Communion (Sacraments)

mass – and to be blessed by the priest. It is only since the Reformation that marriages have taken place inside churches.

In the western countries, the couple usually arrive separately. The man (known as the bridegroom or groom) arrives first, with his 'best man'. He and his family and friends usually sit on the right-hand side of the church. The family and friends of the woman (known as the bride) sit on the left. Then the bride, followed by her attendants (or bridesmaids) walks up the nave to join the groom at the entrance to the chancel.

In the Roman Catholic and many mainstream Protestant Churches, the man and woman (known as the bride and groom) perform the marriage ceremony themselves: they marry one another. The priest or minister is there only to ask (as the law requires) if there is any reason the couple should not marry each other and to declare them man and wife after they have made their vows to each other. They complete their vows with the groom giving the bride her wedding ring, a symbol of their love 'without end'. Some couples exchange rings. The priest then blesses the marriage, and the congregation prays for the couple and their future life together.

A wedding is a time for celebration. The Bible tells us that Jesus went to one wedding in a place called Cana. When the wine ran out, he made more – out of water. This was the first of his miracles (John 2:1-10).

Other Partnerships

The issue of homosexual relationships is a topic of much debate in today's Church. There are statements in the Bible that clearly disapprove of homosexuality. However, some Christians claim that people today have a better understanding of homosexuality and find it more acceptable and believe that such relationships can be loving and, especially if they are permanent, good. Only a few Christian Churches are currently willing to bless civil partnerships (same-sex marriages).

Divorce

If a marriage fails, it may end in divorce. Jewish Law taught that a man could divorce his wife. St Mark's Gospel reports Jesus' teaching on this subject: 'A man who divorces his wife and marries another woman commits adultery. And a woman who divorces her husband and marries another man also commits adultery.'

Jesus also said that, since a man and woman marry in the sight of God, they can only be 'separated' by God.

Because of this, many Christian Churches have taught that divorce and remarriage are always wrong. However, the Orthodox Church has allowed divorce for many centuries 'in cases of extreme distress'. The Roman Catholic Church believes that marriage is a sacrament and therefore unbreakable, but it sometimes allows marriages to be annulled (or 'made nothing') if it can be proved that they were illegal or if the couple have not made love with one another.

In recent times, some Christians have come to feel that (despite Jesus' teaching), if a marriage has failed or fallen apart in some way, it is better for the couple to divorce than to live together unhappily. If they wish to marry someone else and are sorry for any wrongdoing, several Churches will either bless them after a civil ('non-religious') ceremony or allow the remarriage of divorced people to new partners in church.

Christians believe that their religion tells them how they should behave at all times.

The Right Way

The first of the Psalms (the holy songs found in the Old Testament and sung by Christians during church services) talks about those who choose to live a good or moral life.

Happy are those who reject the advice of evil people, who do not follow the example of sinners or join those who have no use for God.

Instead, they find joy in obeying the Law of the Lord and they study it day and night.

They are like trees that grow beside a stream, that bear fruit at the right time, and whose leaves do not dry up. They succeed in everything they do.

This Psalm not only echoes the words of the Ten Commandments but also the teachings of Jesus in his Sermon on the Mount.

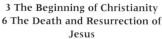

Look it Up

43 Christian Morality

Christians believe that God has made known which things are right and which are wrong. They believe God has done this by giving his people rules for their daily lives – and through the example of Jesus.

For many Christians, the most important rules are the 'Ten Commandments'. These are also the main part of Jewish Law. One of the Jewish holy books called Exodus (which is also part of the Old Testament) tells how God gave the Ten Commandments to one of their early leaders, a man called Moses. The first four commandments are about loving and honouring God; the rest are about respecting other people.

1. You shall have no other gods but me.
2. You shall not make for yourself any idol.
3. You shall not dishonour the name of the Lord your God.
4. Remember the Lord's day and keep it holy.
5. Honour your father and mother.
6. You shall not murder.
7. You shall not commit adultery.
8. You shall not steal.
9. You shall not be a false witness.
10. You shall not covet anything which belongs to your neighbour.

Exodus 20:3–17; Deuteronomy 5:7–21

The first of these commandments was a reminder to the Jews not to behave like other peoples around them who believed in many gods. The second explains why Jews and the early Christians had almost no holy pictures or statues.

These commandments or laws are not only the basis of all Jewish and Christian laws or morality. They have been adopted as part of the law of many countries since Biblical times. As a Jew, Jesus believed in and followed the Ten Commandments.

In ancient times, although the Jews believed there was one true God, other peoples living near them believed in other gods. The Jews were commanded not to worship these 'false gods' – one of whom was called Baal and was said to be the god of rain.

The Two Great Commandments

Once, however, Jesus was asked which was the most important commandment. His answer was:

'*"Love the Lord your God with all your heart, with all your soul, and with all your mind." This is the greatest and the most important commandment. The second most important commandment is like it: "Love your neighbour as you love yourself."*'

Matthew 22:37–39

In fact, Jesus was repeating words from two Jewish holy books (which are also part of the Christian Old Testament), Deuteronomy (6:5) and Leviticus (19:18).

In many ways, these two commandments form a summary of the original Ten Commandments. Either the Ten Commandments or Jesus' summary forms part of many church services.

Over the years, the Christian Church has taught the importance of keeping the Ten Commandments. But during the last 50 years, more importance has been given to Jesus' summary because many Christians feel it more closely reflects his teaching and example. Indeed, the night before he was crucified, he gave his disciples a new commandment: 'Love one another as I have loved you' – so for many Christians what matters most is not simply not 'breaking the rules' (or the Ten Commandments) but actively being a loving person – and as much like Jesus as possible. That is, for example, following the teachings he gave in his Sermon on the Mount.

One of the many things Jesus taught his followers in this sermon was that it is important not to keep up a quarrel with those close to them. If they are angry with (for example) their brother, they should not even pray to God without first going to their brother and making peace with him.

Jesus said a similar thing in the Lord's Prayer, the prayer he taught his followers to say – part of which says, 'Forgive us our sins as we forgive those who sin against us.'

This Christian teaching (that part of living a good or moral life is learning to forgive others, even if they have done wrong) is made clear in one of the parables Jesus told his followers, the Parable of the Prodigal Son. The word 'prodigal' means 'wasteful'.

An olive branch is a symbol of peace. Living peaceably with one another is an important part of Christ's teaching.

The Prodigal Son

A man had two grown-up sons. When he died, his money would be divided between them. But the younger one asked his father if he could have his share straight away. The father said yes.

The younger son went to another country. He soon wasted all his money by spending it carelessly. Then there was a famine in that country. At last, he decided he would have to go back home, ask forgiveness and offer to work as a servant in return for food.

As he neared home, his father saw him – and ran to greet him. The younger son said how sorry he was and that he deserved nothing. The father arranged a feast to celebrate his son's return.

This upset the older son. 'I've worked hard for you,' he told his father. 'My brother's done nothing.'

The father replied that everything he had would be the elder son's – but, even if his younger son had done wrong, it was still right to celebrate his safe return and his new wish to be good.

Santiago de Compostela

One of the first disciples of Jesus was James, the brother of John. Many believe that, after the death of Jesus, he journeyed to Spain to spread the teachings of Jesus there. Later, he became known as the Apostle of Spain and it is believed by many that, after he died, he was buried at a place now known as Santiago de Compostela. From the Middle Ages onwards, many Christians have made a pilgrimage to that town and its cathedral, walking across France and Spain to do so – as these pilgrims have done.

44 Pilgrimage

Christians (like the followers of other faiths) know they can worship and pray anywhere. Churches, chapels and cathedrals are built especially for this purpose. But for some Christians, certain places are 'extra-special' or holy. To journey to one of them may bring a deeper understanding of God or a particular blessing. Such a journey is called a pilgrimage.

The first Christian pilgrimages were probably made in the second century CE. One of the first pilgrimages of which an account survives was one made by Helena, mother of the Roman Emperor Constantine to Jerusalem in the year 326.

By the Middle Ages, pilgrimage was a popular and important activity. For many it was the journey of a lifetime; a 'once-for-all chance' to go somewhere special: either Palestine to visit the places associated with Jesus, or to places important in Christianity – such as Rome where the disciple Peter became the first Bishop and where Paul spent his last days.

For some pilgrims it was not much more than a holiday. True pilgrimage, however, has always been a matter of prayer and faith. In olden times, pilgrimage also involved much hardship and many dangers.

Pilgrims have travelled for all sorts of reasons:
- as a penance (to prove their sorrow at having done something wrong)
- to honour another believer such as a saint
- in the hope of receiving forgiveness or a cure for an illness
- to gain strength or peace of mind.

After the Reformation, many Protestant Christians said pilgrimage was unnecessary, even superstitious, because they felt people were journeying to worship holy places and objects rather than God. With improved travel in the twentieth century, pilgrimage has again become popular. The Holy Land and Lourdes are among the most popular destinations.

Inside the Church of the Holy Sepulchre, Jerusalem – said to be the place where Jesus' body was laid after his crucifixion.

Canterbury

In the year 1170, Canterbury Cathedral (the 'mother church' of the Church of England and the worldwide Anglican Church) became a place of pilgrimage.

Eight years earlier, the King of England, Henry II, had made his friend Thomas Becket Archbishop of Canterbury. Later, the two men quarrelled. The story goes that, in a temper, King Henry said he wished Becket were dead. A group of knights took the king at his word and rode to Canterbury. There they attacked Becket in front of the main altar. A sword crashed through Becket's skull. The knights fled. Becket was dead. It was half past four on the afternoon of 29 December 1170.

Becket's tomb in the cathedral rapidly became a place of pilgrimage. In 1174, King Henry himself came, walking barefoot, to show his sorrow and regret, and allowed himself to be whipped as another sign of his repentance.

For 350 years, Canterbury was one of the most important places of Christian pilgrimage, along with Jerusalem and Rome. Then, in 1538, a later king, Henry VIII, declared Becket had been a traitor and rebel and he had the shrine destroyed. He also took the gold and jewels that decorated the shrine.

Even so, the cathedral still has over one million visitors each year. By no means are all pilgrims or even Christians – but many of the Christians who travel there alone or in church groups see themselves as pilgrims.

Lourdes

In south-west France is a town called Lourdes. There, in 1858, a fourteen-year-old peasant girl called Bernadette Soubirous had a series of 18 dreams or visions. In them, she saw Mary, the mother of Jesus. During one vision, a spring of water appeared out of the ground. People found that this water cured illnesses and even handicaps: Lourdes became a place of pilgrimage, especially for Roman Catholics. Churches, hospitals, hotels and hostels were built for the visitors.

An evening procession of pilgrims outside one of the churches in Lourdes, France.

Look it Up

5 The Ministry of Jesus
7 The First Christians
8 The Life and Journeys of Paul
19 The Reformation

Look it Up

9 The Teachings of Jesus
50 The Fight for Justice Continues

The charitable work of Mother Teresa in India – helping mothers and young babies – is continued by her order of nuns, the Sisters of Charity.

45  Helping Others

Jesus said one of the two great commandments was, 'Love your neighbour as yourself.' He also spoke about the hungry, the homeless and those who are ill: 'Anything you do for one of those, however humble, you do for me.' Christians try to obey these instructions by helping those around them and those in need.

This may mean they go shopping for someone who cannot go out, do jobs for an old person or visit a friend in hospital or even prison. Many churches organize clubs and meetings for the elderly and lonely.

Giving

In olden times, people were expected to give one tenth of all they earned to the Church. This was called a tithe. The Church used some of this money to pay for hospitals and also for schools. (In many countries nowadays, hospitals and schools are paid for by governments, out of money raised by taxes.) Few Christians still 'tithe' their income to their church but all are expected to give some money to their church and to charities.

Heather Reynolds is a nurse and a Christian. She felt it was God's will that she should set up God's Golden Acre to help young ophans who have been affected by HIV/AIDS in South Africa.

Helping in an Emergency

There are many Christian organizations dedicated to providing support to those in desperate need.

The charity Christian Aid began in 1945 to help refugees in Europe at the end of the Second World War. Its motto is 'Life before death' and it now helps people in 60 of the world's poorest countries to find answers to their own problems. For example, in Ethiopia an environment club has been set up to teach children at one school how to look after the land. Because there is so little rain, club members learn how to dig crescent shapes around banana plants. What water does fall can collect there and soak in. Otherwise, it would run away, taking the soil with it. One ten-year-old, Selemon, said, 'Before the club started, we had no fruit. Now we grow different fruits and vegetables and are showing other schools how to do the same.'

From the money Christian Aid receives, 75 per cent is spent on tackling poverty and 11 per cent on campaigns and education. Just 14 per cent is spent on fund-raising and running the charity. Christian Aid knows it cannot do enough by itself to end poverty but works to change trade systems and local laws that cause or maintain poverty.

Christian Charities

Charities are organizations set up to help those in need. Many Christian charities work with the poor and needy in their own countries. For example, some Christian charities run hospices, a home where the life of a person with an illness that cannot be cured or a dying person is made as comfortable and pleasant as possible. Doctors, nurses and carers work to lessen pain and suffering and to try to help overcome the person's fears.

Other Christian charities (such as Christian Aid) help those in poorer countries. They not only send clothes or tins of food abroad but help people in Third World countries to fight disease and hunger themselves and try to persuade politicians to see that wealth is more fairly spread between rich and poor countries.

Christian Aid workers help on farm projects around the world. This one is in Indonesia.

Although the death of a person is a sad event, Christians also believe it is the start of a new and better life.

What Jesus Said

During his life on earth, Jesus often spoke about death. In his Sermon on the Mount, he offered comfort to those who lose a loved one: 'Blessed are those who mourn for they shall be comforted.'

Several times he told his followers that death is not the end of life. For example, he once said, 'Whoever lives and believes in me shall never die' – meaning they shall have everlasting life in heaven. Another time, he said, 'Whoever obeys my teaching shall never die.' (John 8:21).

The coffin is placed in a grave during a funeral service in Ghana, Africa.

46 Death: in Sure and Certain Hope

Christians believe that death is not the end of a life but the start of a new one because of what happened to Jesus after he was crucified: 'On the third day (Easter Day), he rose again.' In this way, he showed his followers that death is not an ending but a way of reaching everlasting life.

So, for Christians, death should not be frightening. But, for the family and friends who are left, it is naturally a sad time because they are saying 'goodbye' to a loved one. Even so, Christians believe that they will meet again in the next life.

The Funeral Service

People of different faiths and people with no faith usually mark the end of a human life on earth with a special ceremony called a funeral.

It is a time for those who are left to show their sorrow and to give thanks for the life that has ended. Christians also want to pray that the person who has died will pass safely into God's care.

Christian funeral services can be quiet and short with only a few members of the family and close friends present – or they can be much larger services with many people attending and with several hymns and other music. A priest, a minister, a relative or friend may speak about what that person achieved in life.

In Roman Catholic and some other Churches, a funeral may be part of a Holy Communion service. In this case it is called a Requiem Mass. (*Requiem* comes from a Latin word meaning 'rest'.)

After the funeral comes the 'committal' when the body is buried or cremated (that is, it is burned).

Burial or Cremation?

All Christians used to believe our earthly bodies would, one day, rise back to life. Because of this belief, they used to be against cremation. This is not the case nowadays as many Christians believe that, when we 'rise again', it will be in another form of life – so it does not matter if the body is cremated.

Burial

The burial may be in a churchyard or in a cemetery. A grave will already have been dug in the ground. The body, in its coffin, is brought to the graveside. More prayers are said and then the body is lowered into the grave. In other cases, the coffin may be put in a vault – a small, windowless room with ledges which is kept locked.

Cremation

In western countries, cremation takes place in a crematorium – a building which looks quite like a church but with curtains or doors through which the coffin will disappear.

After prayers have been said, the coffin (containing the body) is burned in a special furnace. The ashes may be buried or scattered in a place important to the deceased.

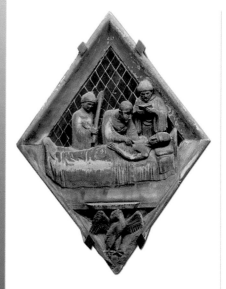

Anointing of the Sick

In the Orthodox and Roman Catholic Churches, people who are suffering from serious illness or are close to death are often anointed with special oil. Prayers are said for the person and then a priest will lay a hand on his or her head and anoint him or her with the oil which has earlier been blessed by a bishop.

This form of anointing may also take place in special healing services or just after a person has died. In the Roman Catholic Church, it is one of the seven sacraments and is often called Holy Unction or Extreme Unction.

Tombstones in memory of the dead in a graveyard in Guatemala.

Look it Up

6 The Death and Resurrection
of Jesus
9 The Teachings of Jesus
34 Holy Communion
47 The Next Life: Heaven
55 The Divided Church

Christians believe that, after death, there is a new, everlasting life.

Purgatory

Since the year 1274, the Catholic Church has taught that those who have died without saying 'sorry' for all their wrongdoings go to a place called 'purgatory'. In purgatory, they may suffer for their sins but will eventually go to heaven. They may be helped on their way to heaven by the prayers of people in this world.

The name 'purgatory' comes from a Latin word meaning 'to cleanse'.

After the Reformation, the Protestant churches rejected the idea of purgatory.

Look it Up

9 The Teachings of Jesus
46 Death: in Sure and Certain Hope
48 The Problem of Suffering
57 Christian Hope

47 The Next Life: Heaven

Some people who do not believe in any religion say that the idea of heaven is just a dream or a hope that death is not the end of everything. Other non-believers say the idea of an 'after-life' in another world is an invention by priests and other people to make us behave in this world. 'If you're good, you'll go to heaven. If not, you'll go to hell.'

But most of the teachers and prophets of the great religions of the world have all taught that death is not the end. Christians believe that this was demonstrated by Jesus when he rose from the dead on the first Easter Day.

Jesus frequently talked about heaven both in his parables and in his Sermon on the Mount. In that sermon, Jesus said that those who love and worship God, who love their neighbours and forgive their enemies will be part of 'the Kingdom of God' or 'the Kingdom of Heaven'. He also warned his followers to be ready to enter heaven at any moment.

That moment, Christians believe, may come on the 'Day of Judgment' – which Jesus also talked about. On this day, Christians believe everyone will be judged as to how well they have lived their lives. Some Christians believe this will happen for everyone on the same 'Day of Judgment' which will happen when the world ends. Others believe it happens for each one of us when we die. We shall then go to heaven – or hell (as Jesus himself said). Catholics also believe in a third 'state' called purgatory.

In the past, Christian teachers described hell as a place where wicked people will suffer everlasting fires and torment. Christians still believe that it is possible to reject God so firmly that one can send oneself to hell but most Christians now place more importance on the loving and forgiving nature of God. They believe he gives us every chance to be with him.

Being 'saved' and reaching heaven is sometimes called 'salvation'.

One Christian was once asked what she thought heaven would be like. She answered, 'I believe I shall be with God in some way. It's not because I'm a good person or because I shall deserve to be there. Or that it's because I'm better than millions of other people. It's because God loves me.'

Angels

Many Christians believe that heaven is also the home of the angels: beings who act as God's messengers. One of the chief angels (or archangels) is said to be called Michael (Jude 9). Some Christians think of him as the protector of the church. Others believe he looks after the souls of people who have died and helps them to reach heaven. They imagine him taking them there by boat – an idea which is remembered in the words of the song 'Michael, Row the Boat Ashore'.

Another angel is known as Gabriel, said to be God's special messenger. The Gospel of St Luke says that it was Gabriel who came to earth to tell Mary that she was to be the mother of Jesus. Because Gabriel brought this message, many people think it was also him who appeared to the shepherds and told them to go and worship the baby Jesus in the manger at Bethlehem.

Like humans, angels are said to be free to choose between doing good and doing wrong. One angel called Lucifer rebelled against God and so lost his place in heaven. He became known as Satan or the Devil. He and his followers are sometimes called 'fallen angels' (2 Peter 2:4; Jude 6).

These angels are from a fresco by the artist Giotto in a church in Assisi, Italy.

Why does a loving God allow suffering?

The Gift of Free Will

Most Christians believe God has given humans the freedom to choose what they do and how they behave. So great is his love for people that God has trusted them – rather like a parent or a teacher saying to a young person, 'Now I'm sure I can trust you…'

God could have made people so that they automatically 'love' him and do exactly what he wished. Then, of course, humans would never do wrong; they would never do wrong or 'sin' – and there would be no cruelty, no misery.

But that kind of 'love' wouldn't be real. If people are to be able to love God genuinely (and to follow in his ways), they must have the freedom or free will to choose how they behave.

Because of this, people have the freedom to do good – or sin.

So Christians, like other people, sometimes sin. These may be 'little' sins such as losing their temper, swearing or being rude. They may be much more serious like bullying – or even very serious such as driving while drunk and causing an accident. For many Christians, the most serious sin is murder because it is the taking away of God's greatest gift of life.

When a huge series of waves or 'tsunami' hit many Asian countries in 2004, millions were left homeless Right, a Christian Aid worker distributes clothing to survivors in Sri Lanka.

48 The Problem of Suffering

One of the main teachings of Christianity is that God loves the world and all the people in it. This leads many people (especially non-Christians) to ask: If God loves us so much, why does he allow so much suffering in the world? Why are there so many wicked and cruel happenings? Why did God let men like Hitler cause so much suffering? Why are innocent children killed in wars or accidents?

The Christian answer is that such things are not the will of God. They are the opposite of what God wants. Evil and accidents only happen because God has given humans free will – to do good or wrong.

Natural Disasters

This does not explain why it doesn't rain in Africa when the crops desperately need it or why earthquakes, typhoons and floods kill hundreds or even thousands of innocent people. So one of the questions people ask about the Christian faith is this: Why does a loving God allow suffering through such natural disasters?

In the past, some Christians answered the question by saying such disasters were punishments for our wrongdoing. Other Christians have said that the purpose of suffering is to make us patient or courageous, that it gives us new understanding.

Christians believe that, on their journey through life, their love for God and their love for one another is tested. But if they continue to trust God (and to care for their loved ones), each soul will mature – and reach heaven.

When St Paul wrote his epistle to the Christians at Rome, he said Christians were to rejoice in suffering because suffering produces endurance and endurance produces character and character produces one of the three great Christian virtues, hope.

Christians also believe it is their duty to help all those who suffer in any way: it is in this way they can show they 'love their neighbour'.

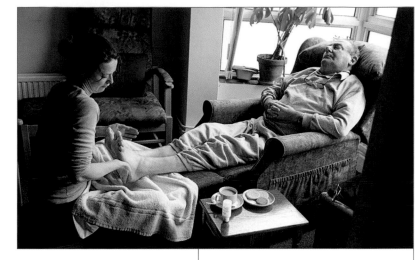

A nurse comforts a patient in St Christopher's Hospice.

The Hospice Movement

In 1967, an English Christian woman called Cicely Saunders (who was both a nurse and a doctor) opened a home called St Christopher's where the suffering and dying could be helped to spend their time in comfort and with the best possible loving care. This home became known as a hospice and, during the twentieth century, more and more hospices were established (many by other Christians). They are places where people's suffering is reduced as much as possible so they can live their final days as fully as possible.

Christ in the World

One message of the Christian Gospel is that, through the incarnation and death of Jesus, God shares in human life and in human suffering – as is shown in this modern parable:

As a Christian lay dying, he saw his life stretch out across the sands of time. For most of his life there was two sets of footprints and he knew that one of them was his own and the other set belonged to Jesus. But then he noticed that, at certain points, there was only one set of footprints. He noticed that this had happened at the saddest moments in his life.

This puzzled him so, when he reached heaven and met Jesus, he asked him, 'Why was it that, when I needed you most, there was only one set of footprints? Why did you leave me?'

Jesus replied, 'My son, I love you and I would never leave you. During those times of suffering when you saw only one set of footprints, it was then that I was carrying you.'

Look it Up

2 The Son of God (Body and Soul)
45 Helping Others
55 The Divided Church

Many Christians have devoted their lives to fighting cruelty and unfairness.

Putting Things Right

Because Jesus told his followers to 'love your neighbour', Christians have tried to obey this instruction by helping those in need. Individual Christians do this personally by helping those around them and by supporting charities.

African American slaves were made to carry heavy bundles of raw cotton from the fields.

49 Christian Reformers

Many Christians have felt called to try to end misery, suffering and injustice not just in their own neighbourhoods but on a wider scale around the world.

Slavery

One injustice that many Christians tried to fight was slavery. Despite Jesus telling his followers to love their neighbours, slavery was widespread for 1,800 years. Many Christians felt it right to buy, own and sell slaves, making them work many hours a day for no pay and sometimes treating them like animals. Slaves were often black people captured by slavers and taken in chains by ship to the Americas. One African who very nearly became a slave in this way was Samuel Adjai Crowther.

As many as 70,000 slaves may have been taken to the Americas in the year 1790 alone. They were seen as a vital unpaid workforce in the cotton plantations. But, by then, some Christians were trying to abolish slavery and all the cruelty linked to it.

By 1804, 'abolitionists' in the northern United States had achieved

One Woman's Fight

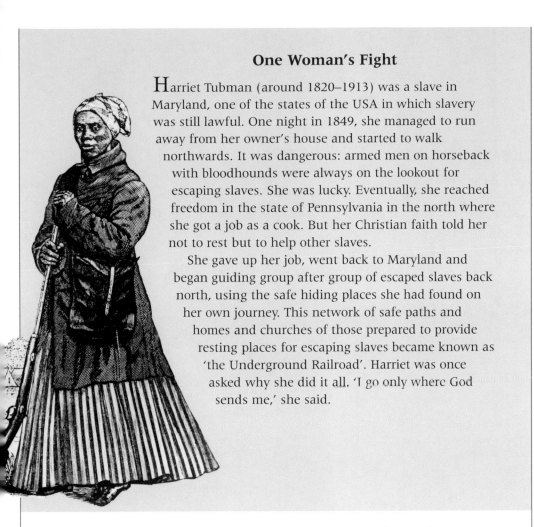

Harriet Tubman (around 1820–1913) was a slave in Maryland, one of the states of the USA in which slavery was still lawful. One night in 1849, she managed to run away from her owner's house and started to walk northwards. It was dangerous: armed men on horseback with bloodhounds were always on the lookout for escaping slaves. She was lucky. Eventually, she reached freedom in the state of Pennsylvania in the north where she got a job as a cook. But her Christian faith told her not to rest but to help other slaves.

She gave up her job, went back to Maryland and began guiding group after group of escaped slaves back north, using the safe hiding places she had found on her own journey. This network of safe paths and homes and churches of those prepared to provide resting places for escaping slaves became known as 'the Underground Railroad'. Harriet was once asked why she did it all. 'I go only where God sends me,' she said.

Elizabeth Fry

Elizabeth Fry (1780–1845) came from a large Quaker family. Besides being the mother of 11 children, she found time to preach at many Quaker meeting houses. When she heard about the conditions in London prisons, she gathered together a number of women Quakers and organised a huge sewing party, making clothes for the prisoners. After visiting one prison, she wrote in her diary about what she had seen. 'There were three hundred women in two rooms. Some had been sentenced to death… I was moved to see two prisoners tearing the clothes from a baby that had just died to clothe one still alive.'

the end of slavery in those states. It was ended in all British countries in 1833 but remained lawful in the southern United States until 1865. Sadly, slavery – including child slavery – still exists in many parts of the world, and Christians are among the many who are campaigning to end it.

Prison Reform

Christians also work for prison reform. Life in prison in those days was often very harsh. Sick prisoners were left to lie (and die) on bare stone floors because there were no beds. Many had only scanty clothing. Sometimes young children lived in prisons, almost naked, simply because they'd been born there.

Elizabeth Fry was one of many Christians who fought to improve conditions for prisoners. For example, she formed a school in the prison for the children of the prisoners and arranged for the women prisoners to do some work which earned them enough to buy clothes, food and soap for themselves and their children. Sadly, many of the prison reforms that were brought about by Christians did not survive.

Look it Up

9 The Teachings of Jesus
21 Differing Denominations
(The Society of Friends)
26 The Church in Africa
45 Helping Others
50 The Fight for Justice Continues

Christians continue to fight poverty, racism and other evils in the world.

Look it Up

Martin Luther King was a Baptist minister and famous civil rights leader in the United States of America. He campaigned against the lack of civil rights for black people by means of non-violent protests. He was assassinated in 1968 but his campaign was, in the end, successful.

50 The Fight for Justice Continues

In recent years (thanks especially to television), millions of Christians in wealthy 'western' countries in Europe, North America and Australasia have become aware of the huge differences in wealth between different parts of the world. Many countries in Europe and North America are very wealthy. At the same time, people in developing countries in west and east Africa, Asia and in central and southern America suffer terrible famine and poverty.

Around the world, many people suffer simply because of the colour of their skin: they are victims of racism.

Many Christians have come to see that, if they are to live their lives following the example of Jesus, then they must bring food and water, medicine and justice to those in need – just as Jesus cared for the people he met.

This has been the work of many Christians over 2,000 years. It is in the last 200 years that it has seemed more important and more urgent.

Poor and homeless children in Santiago, Chile, are fed by members of the Salvation Army.

The Salvation Army

William Booth had been a Methodist minister. He decided he wanted to tell the poor people of London (who rarely went to church) about Jesus. On Christmas morning in 1868, he was preaching in the poorest part of London. He saw hungry people in the street celebrating by getting drunk because they couldn't get food. Next year, he organized 300 free Christmas dinners for them.

Another time in London, he found some homeless men lying in the gutter at night, trying to sleep under newspapers. He and his son rented a warehouse and turned it into a hostel for the homeless.

Other Christians joined him in his mission to help the poor and needy. They said they were 'fighting for God' in their work of salvation: that is, their work of saving people who had nothing in life. They became known as the Salvation Army.

William Booth and his wife Catherine also held meetings in halls they called 'stations' to tell these people about Jesus. They used musical instruments to help the singing and they soon formed bands that played popular music to attract people.

Today, the Salvation Army continues its work of helping others 'in the name of Jesus' but without discrimination. That is, it helps people in need whether they are Christians or not. For example, it helps drug and alcohol addicts overcome their problems, and is one of the largest social care providers in the world – often giving meals to the homeless. It sets to work when there is an emergency such as an earthquake or flood or when there is a major accident. It also runs a Family Tracing Service which tries to find lost relatives and, if possible, to reunite broken families.

Today, the Salvation Army still continues its work of caring for the poor and needy in over 100 countries and it now has about one million members.

Why Does it Matter to Christians?

Christians are not the only people who fight against poverty and injustice. Many would agree that men and women are all born equal. It does not matter in which country they live, what colour their skin is or what sex they are. All deserve an equal chance…

Many would say that no humans are worth less than others because they live in poverty or have a different colour skin…

But…

Christians also believe that each person is loved by God – and therefore should be loved by their neighbours. They should not suffer injustice.

Christians remember how St Paul broke the 'barrier' between Jews and Gentiles, taking the Christian faith to all people, wherever and whoever they were. He once wrote, 'Accept one another… as Christ has accepted you.' (Romans 15:7.) So most Christians believe that they should 'accept' one another – no matter what race they are.

'It is through faith that all of you are God's children in union with Christ Jesus. You were baptized into union with Christ, and now you are clothed… with the life of Christ himself. So there is no difference between Jews and Gentiles, between slaves and free people, between men and women; you are all in one union with Christ Jesus.'

Galatians 3:26–28

Jesus taught that it is better to make peace than to fight. Even so, many Christians have felt it right to go to war.

Poppies grow where land has been disturbed, and have thus become a symbol of peace and remembrance.

A peace mural in Northern Ireland. Sadly, Christians have sometimes fought each other. For example, in Northern Ireland, Protestants and Roman Catholics have fought each other, often in terrible ways. Even through the troubles, however, Christians on both sides also worked for peace.

Look it Up

51 War and Peace

Jesus spoke to his followers about peacemaking during his Sermon on the Mount. 'Blessed are the peacemakers,' he said, 'for they will be called sons of God.' (Matthew 5:9.) Later in that sermon, he said: 'If someone strikes you on the right cheek, turn to him the other also' (Matthew 5:39).

Because of these and other sayings in the Bible, some Christians believe that fighting and violence are always wrong. They refuse to take part in wars and try to put wrongs right by non-violent means. Such people are called pacifists.

Other Christians believe that, sometimes the only way to put things right may be by going to war – just as some leaders (such as Joshua and Gideon) mentioned in the Old Testament had done. For example, in the Middle Ages, many Christians thought it was right to join in the Crusades and fight to capture the 'Holy Land' from Muslims.

In 1939, when Hitler was ruling Germany and invading other neighbouring countries, many Christians thought he was so evil that it was necessary to go to war. Such a war is sometimes called 'a just war' (see right).

Holding torches, peace campaigners in Budapest, Hungary, protest against war. The symbol is that of a campaign to ban nuclear weapons.

In Central and South America, some priests have argued that there is so much poverty and injustice, that the only way to improve the situation is by revolution – which could include fighting and even terrorist activity.

At the start of the twenty-first century, the action of Islamic extremists in New York and other cities led many Christian to start a 'war' against terrorism. Many individual Christians were unhappy about this.

Christian Pacifists

In the same year that the First World War started (1914), a new Pope was elected. He was called Benedict XV and he spoke out against the horrors of that war. Not only was he a worker for peace but he used church money to bring help and comfort to the victims of the war. The various Protestant Churches also did much to help those who were injured or had suffered from the fighting.

During that war, which lasted until 1918, some church people became members of what was known as the Christian Pacifism movement. They refused to take part in the actual fighting but worked as nurses, doctors and stretcher bearers. Many showed great bravery.

Members of the Society of Friends or Quakers are always pacifists. In fact, since the 1960s, many Christians groups have tried to work for world peace. In 1966, for example, the World Council of Churches said that a war should only happen as a very last resort and that the use of nuclear weapons against people not in the fighting forces was always wrong.

A Just War?

The idea of a 'just war' goes back to the time of St Augustine, the bishop of Hippo in North Africa. When his area was threatened by invaders, he said that pacifism was not enough. It was better to fight an invader than to give in if that invader was going to destroy your freedom, including your freedom to worship God.

It is said that seven things must be true before a war can be called just:

✔ What you are fighting for must itself be good or just
✔ That must be the case for as long as the war lasts
✔ The war must lead to something that is good or it must destroy an evil
✔ It must be fought by fair means
✔ It must take place only when all other attempts to put things right have failed
✔ You must be certain you can win the war
✔ The war must aim to bring about peace and justice.

Following the invention of the atom bomb, some Christian preachers (such as Billy Graham) said that a nuclear war using atomic and hydrogen weapons could never be a just war because it would cause so much destruction. Even so, other western Christians said that, as long as the communist Soviet Union had nuclear weapons, it was necessary for other countries to have them for self-defence. Although the world's conflict zones change over time, the debate still continues.

Relations between Christianity and the other great world faiths have sometimes been good, sometimes poor.

The Interfaith Movement

Over the years, more and more people have emigrated from the country of their birth – perhaps to escape persecution or a war, or to find work. This had led to many multicultural societies.

Many Christians are happy to work alongside the different faiths, believing there is good in all religions and that a loving God cares for all people. This is sometimes called the Interfaith Movement. It began in 1893 when a 'Parliament of the World's Religions' was held in Chicago in the United States of America. Since then, many interfaith meetings and discussions have been held at both international and local levels.

Some of these meetings are simply for ordinary people to get to know each other. Other meetings involve religious leaders trying to work for world peace and to end poverty, hunger and unnecessary sickness.

52 Christianity and Other Faiths

Near the end of his life on earth, Jesus told his disciples that when the Holy Spirit came to them, they would 'be filled with power, and you will be witnesses for me… to the ends of the earth' (Acts 1:8). So, even in its earliest days, followers of the Christian faith journeyed to distant countries to persuade people to become members of the Church.

Much later, in the 1500s and also in the nineteenth and twentieth centuries, there was more 'missionary' activity. In some cases, these Christian missionaries were trying to persuade people of no faith or those who followed native or tribal religions to become Christians. In other cases, they were hoping to convert people who already believed in one of the other great world faiths to Christianity.

This was because some Christians have placed much importance on these words of Jesus: 'No one goes to the Father (God) except by me.' (John 14:6.) They have believed that people will not reach heaven unless they become Christian.

Conflict Between the Faiths

As a result of this, some Christian missionaries tried to force their beliefs on the peoples they met. Some missionaries even offered food and medical care only to those who would become Christian.

Members of different world faiths join in prayer in London, England in 2005.

Christians and Jews

Christians have not always had good relations with the Jewish people. For many centuries, some Christians blamed the Jews for the death of Jesus and treated them very badly. Indeed, ever since the Jews were scattered from their homeland by the Romans and forced to live in European countries, they were often treated as second-class citizens.

Nowadays, relations between the two faiths are much better.

Christianity and Islam

The second largest faith in the world (by numbers) is Islam. Its followers are also encouraged to spread the teachings of that religion around the world. As they tried to make countries Muslim, they inevitably sometimes came into conflict with Christianity. These conflicts led to the Crusades and to Muslim rule in Spain for many years. Much later, as the British empire grew and Britain took control of Muslim countries in the Middle East and Asia, there was more conflict.

In recent times, there have been new conflicts between Muslims and Christians. In particular, some Muslims feel that western (or Christian) countries are again trying to interfere in 'their part of the world'.

It is impossible to work out exactly how many followers each religion has but these are approximate estimates:

Followers of many faiths celebrate together in Kathmandu.

Interfaith Services

In recent years, Christians have begun to welcome followers of the other religions to their services on special occasions.

At important state occasions, leaders of various faiths may be invited to take part in what is mainly a Christian service in order to show love and friendship between all believers.

Christianity	2,100 million
Islam	1,300 million
Hinduism	900 million
Buddhism	376 million
Chinese traditional religions	394 million
African traditional religions	100 million
Sikhism	23 million
Judaism	12 million
Other primal, native religions	300 million
Atheism (those who say there is no God) and agnostics (those who are unsure)	1,100 million

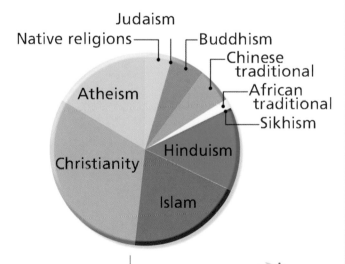

Look it Up

In a changing world, Christians have to decide where they stand on environmental and medical matters.

How Long Do You Want to Live?

Thanks to discoveries made by scientists, many diseases and illnesses that were once 'incurable' can now be prevented or treated.

This raises a number of questions. If parents are unable to have children, should they be allowed to use new 'artificial' methods of creating life by using cells or genes taken from someone else?

What should be done if it is discovered that an unborn child is almost certain to grow up with a serious illness in later life?

Everyone wants to end terrible diseases such as smallpox and cholera – but what happens if most diseases can be overcome? How long will we want to live?

None of these questions was being asked in biblical times. All Christians can do is to think how Jesus, the great healer, might have answered each one.

Look it Up

5 The Ministry of Jesus
42 Marriage
43 Christian Morality
48 The Problem of Suffering
55 The Divided Church

53 Questions for Christians

In the last 100 years, we have seen many inventions and changes. Cars and aircraft have altered the way we travel and the speed at which we travel. Radio, television and mobile phones have given us new ways to get in touch with each other. We have begun to explore space. Many once-deadly diseases can now be prevented or cured. We live longer. And there are more of us. Many more of us.

All these changes raise questions for Christians.

The Environment

During the last 20 years, more and more people have become aware of the dangers to the earth's environment. Global warming, pollution, the destruction of forests, using too many of the world's natural resources too quickly… All these things are happening because of human greed or thoughtlessness. We are dirtying our planet.

Christians are among those who are now tackling these problems. Several churches in the USA have begun to campaign to prevent toxic waste sites being built near their homes. Around the world, other Christians are working to limit the pollution of the land, water and air.

They are doing this partly because they know it is good for the planet and for those who live on it (including themselves). They also do it because they believe God has given them the job of looking after his world; they are his 'stewards' who must look after his creation.

The Population

The population of the world has grown rapidly in the last 100 years and is set to grow steadily in the future.

In 1900, it is estimated the world's population was about 1,600 million.

In 2005, it is estimated the world's population was about 6,500 million.

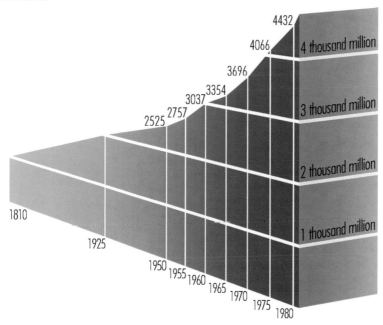

With the growth in the world's population, some Christians are now asking whether parents should be allowed to have as many children as they like – or must they limit the size of their families?

The world's largest Church, the Roman Catholic Church, teaches that artificial contraception is always wrong. Other Christians question this.

Abortion

Another question that has been talked about more in recent times is abortion. Abortion is the ending of a pregnancy at some stage between conception and birth.

Many Christians (sometimes called 'pro-life' Christians) believe abortion is always wrong. They say that a baby is a human being – even when it is in its mother's womb. To end that life is always wrong. Pope John Paul II called it murder.

Other 'pro-choice' Christians believe that sometimes, sadly, it is better to end a pregnancy in its early stages than to allow the unborn foetus to grow. This may be because doctors can tell the baby will be born with very serious medical problems; because the pregnancy may harm the mother or because pregnancy happened as a result of rape.

Medical Debates

Modern developments have raised many other issues for Christians.

- Should we do research on animals to improve human health?
- Should parents be allowed to choose the sex of their baby?
- Is 'cloning' or artificially creating life against God's will?
- How far should Christians go to protest against (or try to stop) something they feel is wrong? For example, if Christians feel abortion is very wrong, should they attack doctors or clinics where abortions happen?
- What should be done with serious criminals such as murderers? Is the death penalty against the commandment 'You shall not murder'?

Christians take these questions seriously but different Christians reach different answers.

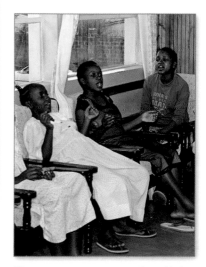

Young pregnant women rest and worship in a Christian care home in Nairobi, Kenya. The care offered provides a way for them to keep their babies.

Respect for the Bible

All Christians respect the Bible but they differ in how much they can interpret its teachings to deal with present day knowledge and understanding.

Fundamentalists may quote this passage from Revelation to defend their choice of taking the Bible literally:

'I, John, solemnly warn everyone who hears the prophetic words of this book: if anyone adds anything to them, God will add to his or her punishment the plagues described in this book. And if anyone takes anything away from the prophetic words of this book, God will take away from them their share of the fruit of the tree of life and of the Holy City, which are described in this book.'

Revelation 22:18–19

For some Christians, the Old Testament story of a man called Jonah being swallowed by a very large fish for three days is literally true. For others, it is simply a story warning what may happen to those who disobey God's commands and promising that God will forgive wrongdoers.

54 Fundamentalism

Fundamentalists are Christians who believe that every part of the Bible is literally true. That is, when Genesis, the first book in the Old Testament, says God created the world in six days, it means exactly that. They do not believe the view held by other Christians who say the first chapter of Genesis is a kind of poem explaining that God slowly created the world step by step. They also believe that all the miracles performed by Jesus happened exactly as they are described and that there is not a scientific explanation for them which people did not understand at the time.

Fundamentalists insist that true Christians believe four other things:
• Mary was a virgin when she gave birth to Jesus
• Jesus' body came back to life on the first Easter Day (that is, his friends and disciples did not imagine it)
• Only God's chosen will reach heaven
• Jesus will, one day, come back to earth as a living being.

Fundamentalist Christians do not all belong to one particular denomination but may be found among the members of several of the Protestant Churches. They usually keep very strictly to the teachings of the Bible.

The word 'fundamentalist' was first used in 1920 by an American journalist called Curtis Lee Laws. He used it to describe 'anti-modern' Protestants who preached the literal truth of the Bible and the sinfulness of humankind – and who described these ideas as the 'fundamentals' of the Christian faith.

Fundamentalist Christians have a strong, unshakable faith and often show great courage. They remain fiercely committed to their established view of morality and can be unwilling to consider new ideas or evidence.

Fundamentalism became popular in the United States when communism was seen as a threat to the western world. During the 1950s, there were many famous evangelical and fundamentalist preachers, such as Billy Graham; 20 or 30 years later, new fundamentalist televangelists used the medium of television to preach their beliefs.

In recent years, fundamentalism has again become very popular in the United States of America and, during George W. Bush's presidency, many important political jobs were given to fundamentalist Christians.

Look it Up

Evolution or Darwinism?

In 1859, an English scientist called Charles Darwin published a book in which he argued that all the various forms of life (including humans) had gradually developed or evolved over thousands of years. Because this seemed to go against the teaching of Genesis, it infuriated many Christians at the time.

Since then, many Christians have come to see the scientific truth of much of what he says and accept the idea that although God did not create the world in six days (as Genesis says), the world and all that is in it are still God's work.

Fundamentalist Christians who hold the Bible to be literally true do not accept this.

The disagreement became very public in 1920. Fundamentalists had been campaigning against the teaching in schools of Charles Darwin's theory and this campaign led to laws being passed in 11 states, outlawing 'Darwinism'. One of the states was Tennessee. A man called John T. Scopes, who taught at a school in Dayton in that state, broke the law. He was prosecuted, found guilty and fined $100. The law in Tennessee was not changed until 1967.

Darwin based his book on what he saw during a voyage round the world – which included a visit to the Galapagos Islands in the South Pacific.

The Church is now divided not so much by differences between the denominations as by differences between 'traditional' and 'liberal' Christians.

Who are the Evangelicals?

The word 'evangelical' has various meanings.

An 'evangelist' is any Christian who spreads the teachings of Jesus – just as the original evangelists were those early Christians who first spread the faith either by preaching or by writing down the news about Jesus. (The writers of the four Gospels are often called the Four Evangelists.)

'Evangelical' is also often used to describe any Christian or any church which believes especially in the importance of the Bible. Pentecostalists, Fundamentalists and members of some other Protestant Churches may describe themselves as evangelicals. Many (but not all) evangelical Christians hold traditional beliefs.

Young Evangelical Christians taking Holy Communion at a World Youth Day in Rome.

55 The Divided Church

Over the centuries, the Christian Church has been divided into different denominations. These denominations have kept apart for various reasons. They may have wanted to worship in different ways. They may have disagreed as to whether the pope should be head of the Church or not. They may have held and still hold different beliefs about Holy Communion or baptism.

In recent years, there has been a change. Nowadays, it is sometimes easier to think of Christians as being divided not between the denominations but between 'traditional' Christians and 'liberal' Christians. This is partly because both traditional and liberal Christians may be found in the same denomination.

* Traditional Christians usually believe that what is written in the Bible is true for all time and should not be altered. Fundamentalist Christians are almost always traditional in their beliefs. Roman Catholic traditionalists also accept all the teachings of their leaders, especially of the popes.

* Liberal Christians usually believe it is right to work out what Jesus' teachings mean for today and how they can best put them into practice in the modern world.

In 2006, Katharine Jefferts Schori became the first woman to be elected bishop of an Episcopal (or Anglican) Church.

Women in the Church

Over the years, Christians have used sentences or 'verses' from the Bible to keep women from positions of importance – even in the home. One verse such Christians quote is this: 'Wives, submit to your husbands… for a husband has authority over his wife' (Ephesians 5:22–23).

So, for most of the 2,000 years since the Church began, women were kept from positions of leadership in the Church. There were no women priests, certainly no women bishops. Eventually, some denominations allowed women to become ministers and preachers. One of the first was the Society of Friends – in which Elizabeth Fry was a leading speaker. Nowadays, large numbers of Christians (and certainly all liberal Christians) believe women deserve equality with men.

However, the Roman Catholic and Orthodox Churches remain firmly opposed to women priests. They do so for various reasons. They say that Jesus was a man and when the priest celebrates the Mass or Eucharist, he is taking the place of Jesus. Only a man can do this. Others oppose women priests because Jesus chose only men as his closest disciples.

Those in favour of women priests say that the main thing about Jesus is that he was God become human, not God become a man. They also point to the fact that Jesus had many close women friends and followers – and that things have changed over the years. Women now have the chance to do all sorts of jobs that once were done only by men. It's only fair they should be able to become priests.

Despite their Church's teachings, some Roman Catholics now feel women should be priests. Roman Catholics are also divided on matters such as whether priests should be allowed to marry.

Because of what Paul wrote in one of his letters, some Protestant Churches do not allow women to preach or to be in charge of congregations: 'I do not allow them to teach' (1 Timothy 2:12). Others disagree, pointing out that he also said, 'There is no difference… between men and women; you are all one in union with Christ Jesus' (Galatians 3:28).

Euthanasia

Another issue that divides Christians is euthanasia.

Euthanasia means helping a person who is terminally ill (that is, with no hope of getting better) to end their life comfortably and easily. Many Christian Churches (including the Roman Catholic and Anglican Churches) disagree with this. They believe terminally ill people need to be cared for and given pain relief; not helped to die.

Some liberal Christians believe it is a loving act to help end the life of someone who is suffering and who feels ready to die.

Look it Up

Despite their disagreements, most Christian Churches hope they will one day be again united.

Ecumenism

The word 'ecumenical' comes from Greek and means worldwide or universal. The Churches talk of ecumenism or ecumenical events to describe projects or church services that bring the different church groups or denominations together.

Week of Prayer for Christian Unity

Christians around the world join in this annual week of ecumenical prayer for unity, which is held in January in most countries. (A few observe it at Pentecost.) The week is now planned jointly by the World Council of Churches and a Roman Catholic council for Christian unity.

The Church of South India was formed in 1947. It brought together Anglicans, Methodists, Presbyterians and other Protestants in one united Church. Its members now worship together and in the same way.

56 Towards Christian Unity?

People outside the Christian Churches often wonder why there are so many different Churches and why Christians cannot agree among themselves. 'Why should I join something when even its members can't agree with themselves?' they ask. It is a good question, especially as Jesus himself prayed that all his followers 'should be one' – that is, united (John 17:20–21).

Ever since the Roman and Orthodox Churches split in 1054, the Church has continued to break up into more and more separate groups or denominations. Over the centuries, these splits (leading to disagreements, quarrels and even wars) have been one of the saddest parts of the Christian story. Until about 60 years ago, Roman Catholics were not even allowed to say the Lord's Prayer with Protestants.

These disagreements have not just been between the various Churches. People in the same Church may disagree with one another. For example, some Anglicans believe that people may remarry in church after having been divorced. Others do not. Some Roman Catholics believe women should be allowed to become priests even though their Church says they cannot.

Brother Roger is here seen at an evening service in Hamburg, Germany.

'That Little Springtime'

In a village called Taizé in France, there is a small church built in the 1100s. Going into it from bright sunshine is like going into total darkness. It's a very peaceful place in which to think and to worship in silence.

Taizé is also home to a very special Christian community and is a place of pilgrimage. Every year, thousands of young Christians from all denominations go there to live in tents and huts, to eat and worship together in a huge tent and to learn more about their faith.

The Taizé community was started at the end of the Second World War by a Swiss monk, Brother Roger. He moved there in 1940 and started helping refugees. After the war, he was joined by others. Also known as brothers, they came from Roman Catholic, Anglican, Lutheran and other Protestant Churches and their aim was to start a place where young people from all branches of the Christian Church could join together in worship and unity.

Because it was a place of peace and hope, Pope John Paul II once described it as 'that little springtime in the Church'.

Sadly, Brother Roger was stabbed to death in 2005 in the prayer tent at Taizé. Even so, it remains a place of peace and young people still spread its message of Christian hope and unity around the world.

The World Council of Churches

Over the last 50 years, the various Churches have started to work and worship together far more than they did in the past.

One way they have tried to overcome their differences and quarrels is in the World Council of Churches (WCC). It was formed in 1948 and has its headquarters in Switzerland. Its members include Orthodox, Anglican, Methodist, Baptist and Pentecostal Churches. The Roman Catholic Church is not a full member but joins in some of the discussions.

The WCC encourages its member Churches to work together to fight poverty, injustice, racism, famine and illnesses such as HIV/AIDS. It also works for peace – for example, between Israel and its neighbours.

The logo of the World Council of Churches.

Look it Up

16 The Orthodox Churches
19 The Reformation
20 Differing Denominations
44 Pilgrimage

Paul said Christians should believe in Jesus and love each other. He also told them to hope.

Messages of Hope in the Bible

In Revelation, the writer of that book, John, describes his vision of the new heaven and the new earth:

'The first heaven and the first earth disappeared, and the sea vanished. And I saw the Holy City, the new Jerusalem, coming down out of heaven from God, prepared and ready... I heard a loud voice speaking from the throne: "Now God's home is with human beings! He will live with them, and they shall be his people. God himself will be with them, and he will be their God. He will wipe away all tears from their eyes. There will be no more death, no more grief or crying in pain. The old things have disappeared."'

Revelation 21:1–4

Look it Up

9 The Teachings of Jesus
10 The Teachings of Paul
33 Private and Public Prayer

57 Christian Hope

In one of the letters or epistles Paul wrote to Christians at Corinth, he taught the importance of three things. One of these was hope.

For all Christians, hope is important. They keep their faith in the hope of 'life everlasting, through Jesus Christ'. They also live their lives and work in the hope of making the world a better place and more like the sort of world that would please God. As they pray in the Lord's Prayer, 'Your will be done.'

Sometimes Christians feel disappointed that more people do not join their faith or believe the things they believe. The numbers of those going to church in Europe has fallen considerably in recent years. But in Africa, Asia and Latin America it is another story. More and more people are becoming Christian.

Christianity began in a small Middle Eastern country on the edge of Asia. For 1,900 years, it was mainly a European religion. Now, far more Christians live in the developing world than Europe – and there are far more non-white than white Christians.

On World Youth Day in the year 2000, young pilgrims celebrate the Easter message.

The Pilgrim's Progress: **John Bunyan**

John Bunyan lived in England from 1628 to 1688. He earned his living by travelling from village to village mending pots and pans and other items. He had strong Christian beliefs and wanted to preach his faith. But, although this was after the Reformation, ordinary people weren't allowed to preach in public places – which is what he did.

As a result, he was imprisoned for preaching without a licence – four times. While in prison in Bedford, he wrote the first part of one of the most famous Christian books outside the Bible.

It's called *The Pilgrim's Progress* and tells the story of a man called Christian who goes on a long journey through places such as the City of Destruction (a place of noise and anger) and a slimy, filthy patch of mud called the Slough of Despond. He meets good friends such as Faithful and Hopeful and, by keeping to the Straight and Narrow Path, he eventually reaches the Heavenly City.

The Pilgrim's Progress is a parable because Christian's journey represents every Christian's journey through life with its temptations and troubles – until he or she reaches the Heavenly City.

This picture was created for a nineteenth-century edition of Bunyan's story to show Christian's journey from the City of Destruction to the Heavenly City.

Christianity Today

• There are over 2,000 million Christians in the world today.

• Half of them are Roman Catholics – and half the Roman Catholics live in Central and South America.

• The Orthodox Churches have about 300 million members.

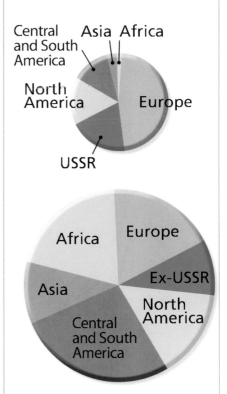

These pie charts show the distribution of Christians in each continent as a proportion of the total population of the world in 1900 (above) and 2000 (below). The circles are in proportion to the total population.

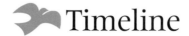

Timeline

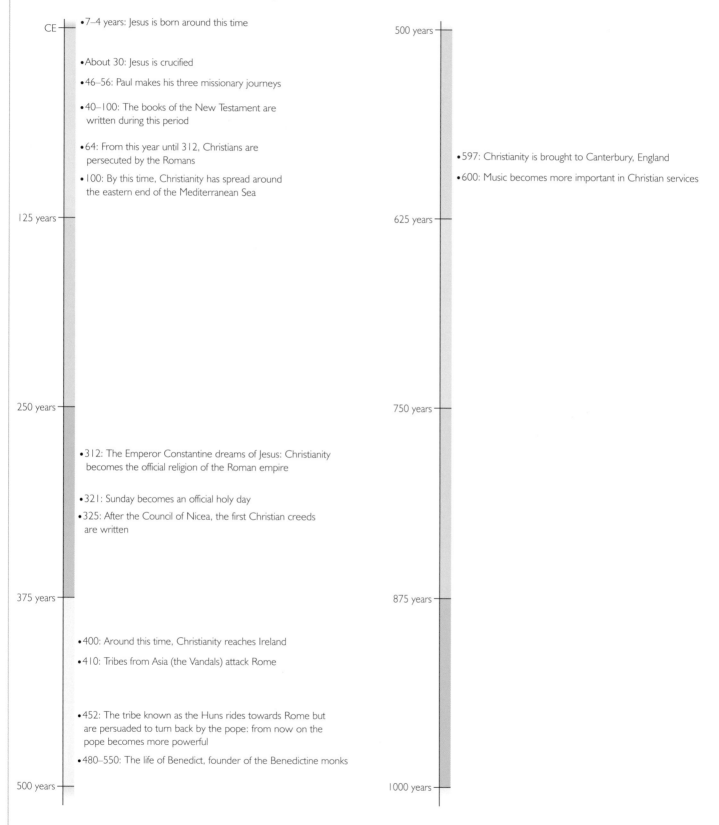

CE

•7–4 years: Jesus is born around this time

•About 30: Jesus is crucified

•46–56: Paul makes his three missionary journeys

•40–100: The books of the New Testament are written during this period

•64: From this year until 312, Christians are persecuted by the Romans

•100: By this time, Christianity has spread around the eastern end of the Mediterranean Sea

125 years

250 years

•312: The Emperor Constantine dreams of Jesus: Christianity becomes the official religion of the Roman empire

•321: Sunday becomes an official holy day

•325: After the Council of Nicea, the first Christian creeds are written

375 years

•400: Around this time, Christianity reaches Ireland

•410: Tribes from Asia (the Vandals) attack Rome

•452: The tribe known as the Huns rides towards Rome but are persuaded to turn back by the pope: from now on the pope becomes more powerful

•480–550: The life of Benedict, founder of the Benedictine monks

500 years

500 years

•597: Christianity is brought to Canterbury, England

•600: Music becomes more important in Christian services

625 years

750 years

875 years

1000 years

1000 years		1500 years	

• 1054: The Catholic and Orthodox Churches split

• 1095–1099: The first Crusade

• 1181 or 1182–1226: The life of Francis, founder of the Franciscan friars

• 1377: The Vatican (in Rome) becomes the headquarters of the Roman Catholic Church

• 1485 onwards: Christianity spreads to Central and South America

1125 years

1250 years

1375 years

1500 years

• 1510: Martin Luther visits Rome

• 1517: The start of the Reformation: Luther makes public his criticisms of the Roman Catholic Church

• 1526: The first Bible in English is printed

• 1533: Henry VIII, King of England and Wales, breaks with the Roman Catholic Church, creating the Church of England, later to be part of the worldwide Anglican or Episcopalian Church

• 1540s: The beginnings of the Calvinist Church in Switzerland

• 1609: The beginning of the Baptist Church in the Netherlands

• 1612: The Baptist Church spreads to England

• 1626: The completion of the rebuilding of St Peter's Church, Rome

• 1639: The first Baptist church in America is founded at Providence on Rhode Island

• 1650s: The start of the Society of Friends (Quakers)

• 1693: The Amish Church begins in America

• 1722 onwards: The development of the Moravian Church

• 1726 onwards: The First Great Awakening in America

• 1780s: Methodism begins as a group within the Church of England but in 1784 becomes a separate Protestant Church

• 1800 onwards: The Second Great Awakening in America

• 1804: The start of the British and Foreign Bible Society

• 1816: The American Bible Society is founded

• 1850 onwards: Christian missionaries travel widely in Africa

• 1865: The Salvation Army is founded

• 1900: By now the Bible has been translated into 100 languages

• 1900 onwards: Rapid growth of Christianity in Africa

• 1906: The Pentecostal Movement begins in the United States of America

• 1920s: The development of Fundamentalism

• 1940s: The Cursillo Movement develops in Spain

• 1945: The founding of the charity Christian Aid

• 1949: The formation of the World Council of Churches

• 1960s: Rapid growth of the Pentecostal Churches

• 1968: The start of 'Liberation Theology' to help the poor in Central and South America

• 1968: Assassination of Martin Luther King

• 1970s: Christians persecuted in Uganda

1625 years

1750 years

1875 years

2000 years

Events in the history of the Orthodox Churches are shown in chapter 24.

Index

Page numbers in *italics* refer to illustrations.